Killer Movies: The Essential Thrillers

Stephen Hoover

Killer Movies: The Essential Thrillers

Copyright © 2013 by Stephen Hoover

Library of Congress Control Number: 2013922640

Book design by: Cat Stewart

Cover design by: 2Faced Design

All rights reserved. No part of this book may be used or reproduced in any manner whatsoever including Internet usage, without written permission of the author.

ISBN: 978-0-9897465-6-4

Dedicated to the Master of Suspense, Alfred Hitchcock

Table of Contents

CHAPTER 1: WHAT IS A THRILLER? 1
   Essential Elements 1
   Differences with Other Genres 5
CHAPTER 2: BEYOND GENRES: WHAT MAKES A THRILLER WORK? 9
   Setting 10
   Infinite Variety, Unending Suspense 11
   The Players 12
CHAPTER 3: THE VILLAIN 15
   The Sympathetic Villain 15
   The Secret Society 16
   The Syndicate 17
   The Madman 18
   The Brute 19
   Evil Incarnate 20
   The Darker Half 21
   Classy, Cultured and Pure Evil 23
CHAPTER 4: KNOW THY ENEMY: EVIL TROPES IN THRILLERS 25
   A Framework for Understanding: Beliefs and Behaviors ... 31
   Wickedly Evil 33
   Categorizing Evil 33
CHAPTER 5: THE PROTAGONIST 39
   Who Wants to Be a Hero? 40
   The Anti-Hero 41
   The Reformed Criminal 42
   Man, Woman or Both on the Run 42
   Just Plain Naïve 43
   Good vs. Evil vs. Reality 44
BONUS CHAPTER: SYMPATHY FOR THE DEVIL 45
   Sympathy 46
   There But for the Grace… 47
   We're Not So Different… 49
M: SOME OF THE ROOTS OF THE THRILLER (1931) 53
   Plot and Story 53
   The Shark in the Water 54

    Paranoia *55*
    The Fin above the Water *56*
    The Investigation: Instant Tension *58*
    More than Just Police Technology *59*
    Enjoying the Film *61*
    The Absence of Effects and Thrillers *61*
GASLIGHT: DRIVEN INSANE (1944) *63*
    The Plot and Setup *63*
    The Isolation Treatment *66*
    Mental Games *67*
    Paula Gets Her Revenge *68*
    Why This Film Works *69*
REAR WINDOW: A VIEW TO A KILLER (1954) *73*
    The Plot and Setup *73*
    Involvement and Voyeurism *75*
    The Complexity of Jefferies *77*
    Lisa Is Awesome *78*
    Doyle *80*
    Miss Lonelyheart *81*
    Hitchcock Reminds You to Fear Him *82*
    Why This Film Works *84*
BONUS CHAPTER: THE YELLOW WALLPAPER *87*
    The Plot *88*
    The Descent *89*
    How the Trope Plays Out Today *90*
NORTH BY NORTHWEST: THE PERFECT SPY THRILLER (1959) *93*
    A Brilliant Setup for a Brilliant Film *93*
    Why This Setup Works *96*
    The Plot Thickens *97*
    The Plane Scene *98*
    We're All Roger Thornhill *99*
BONUS CHAPTER: WHO WAS HITCHCOCK? *100*
    Hitchcock's Background *100*
    A Complex Man *101*
    Style *102*
    The Average Guy *102*
    Why They Endure *103*
FATAL ATTRACTION: SEXUAL PARANOIA IN THE AGE OF AIDS (1987) *105*

The Plot and Setup	105
The Age of AIDS	106
You Cannot Make this Go Away	108
When It Gets Dark It Gets Very Dark	109
The Climax You Won't Forget	109
Why This Film Works	110
JACOB'S LADDER: TERROR, MADNESS AND CONSPIRACY (1990)	**113**
The Plot	114
Tapping Into Insanity in Thrillers	117
The Right Protagonist	118
Farther Down	118
The Conspiracy Revealed	119
It All Comes Clear	120
MISERY: THE CONTAINED THRILLER (1990)	**123**
Plot and Setup	123
Paul Sheldon's Ordeal	125
Annie Wilkes	127
It Just Keeps Getting Worse	128
The Tensest Scenes	129
The Final Confrontation	130
Why This Film Works	131
THE SILENCE OF THE LAMBS (1991): KILLERS, MADNESS AND BEYOND	**133**
The Plot	133
Delving into the Darkness	135
How Is He Possibly Charming?	136
Buffalo Bill	137
Transgenderism and Serial Killers in Thrillers	139
Clarice Gets Her Killer	140
Why This Film Works	141
SE7EN: DARK, GRIMY AND TERRIFYING (1995)	**142**
The Setting and Setup	143
It's Always Raining	144
Twisting the Protagonist	145
The Story	145
The Killer	147
The Setup	149
The Procedural Element	150
Telltale Signs of Psychosis/Psychopathy	151

    Not a Happy Ending 152
MEMENTO (2000): THE CYCLE OF MADNESS.. 157
    The Plot and Setup 157
    Making Sense of the Film 158
    Leonard's Quest 159
    The Femme Fatale 160
    How This Film Succeeds 161
    The Plot Unfolds, but Not Clearly 162
    Mental Illness in Thrillers 164
TAKEN (2008) 167
    The Setup 167
    The Bad Guys Are Bad, the Good Guys Are Worse 169
    The Violence 170
    The Drama Unfolds 171
    Why This Film Works 175
FOR FURTHER SWEATING.. 177

Introduction

Thriller films are hard to pigeonhole. They can cross genres but they still retain their essential character. They are sometimes more terrifying than any horror movie around, but lack the fantasy elements of that genre. In some regards, they are horror films for adults, but they are so much more.

Thrillers are sometimes about ordinary people in extraordinary situations and sometimes about the menace that lurks in what seems mundane. They are sometimes globe-hopping spy adventures and sometimes take place in one room.

Thriller films include some of the best examples of filmmaking on the whole. The genre has been explored by and defined by some of the finest writers, directors and actors in the filmmaking business.

Whether you're looking for subtle scares or feel like watching an entire movie through your fingers, dreading what comes next, there's likely a thriller out there that offers exactly what you're looking for and, probably, much more.

This book gives a list of some of the best thrillers out there and includes some that tend not to get the attention they deserve as films of the genre. For fans, it should offer some new films to give a chance. For those new to this genre, it's a great starting point and the films listed are likely to include more than one that will get you hooked.

Whether the genre is new or old to you, however, you're sure to get some very pronounced anxiety from the films listed, and to enjoy some very cerebral, satisfying tales on top of it.

Chapter 1

What Is a Thriller?

A thriller film may be projected onto a screen, but, if it's good, it will burn into your psyche forever. It will make you afraid to stay at that hotel in the mountains, afraid that you might be losing your mind, and most of all, it will make you afraid that the darkest place of all is within you, or in the person right next to you.

Essential Elements

Thriller films share some of their essential elements with other film genres and, in fact, with good storytelling on the whole. A thriller film, when done properly, elicits a feeling of tension and sometimes nearly unbearable anxiety in the viewer. This sometimes climaxes with a moment of complete terror, but thrillers can be subtler than that.

FindMeanAuthor.com, quoting from the *International Thriller Writers*, defines the genre as one that causes a rush of emotions in the viewer, and most of those emotions are anxious ones.

Style
Thrillers can be subtle, but are also sometimes anything but. The pace can be a slow burn, fast from the start or anything in-between.

Because thriller movies take place in so many different settings, they have many different styles between them, aesthetically speaking. They can take place in the slickest, most high-tech spy lairs or out in the country, miles from where anyone can hear you scream, as the saying goes. They can involve the lives of the rich and famous—or infamous—just as they can involve the life of someone hiding out in a cabin by a lake, on the lam from the law, their enemies or themselves.

Alfred Hitchcock, who we focus on in later chapters, set some of the standards for the thriller genre. One of his favorite ways to build tension was to move the camera around the room in a way that allowed the audience to participate more fully in the story. This technique takes the audience out of the role of passive observers and turns them into active participants. In moments where the anxiety is particularly high, this technique can be very effective at drawing the viewer in, sometimes making them justly afraid of what the camera is about to reveal to them, and how that's going to make them feel.

In some cases, the directors profiled in later chapters may have distinctive styles and techniques that people will recognize as having become common elements in thriller movies. Kubrick's technical perfectionism, for example, was put to good use giving the viewer unique and unexpected access to what was going on at the Overlook Hotel in *The Shining*. He used cameras that tracked the characters as they moved through the hotel's hallways, offering tension-building points of view, even to the point of using what was new technology at the time to accomplish certain shots. Most audiences would agree that the result was an unnerving one, to say the least.

Tension and Suspense

One of the things that tend to make good thrillers stand out is that they excel in the storytelling aspects of film. This gets the audience more involved with the characters. When you begin to like or even to just have compassion for someone, it's a lot more terrifying to watch them lose their mind, be threatened by brutal criminals or be the victim of an even more mysterious and brutal sort of menace.

Writer's Digest gives a good summary of some of the most effective ways to build tension in storytelling, and they all play roles in thriller films from all eras.

Time is oftentimes set up as a foe. The protagonist has a limited amount of time to complete a given task. For instance, in the film *Se7en*, much of the tension relies on the audience knowing that the killer will strike again if the protagonists don't find him first. Time can be used in exactly the opposite way, however. For instance, in the aforementioned film *The Shining*, the tension is contributed to by the fact that the characters—along with the audience—are isolated from the outside world during the brutal winters. They have too much time, not too little.

A good thriller can use any of many different techniques to build suspense, and the best use many different ones to put the audience at unease.

Variations

The thriller genre has many subtypes that are popular and that can all be very strong examples of the form in their own ways. They include:

Crime Thrillers: *Chinatown*, for example, is a fine example of a crime thriller. *Midnight Express* is another. *The Usual Suspects* is a good example of using tension to distract the audience from a twist that seemed obvious when it was eventually revealed. This is a familiar, effective and really quite satisfying technique.

Psychological Thrillers: These oftentimes intersect with horror thrillers, particularly if madness is driving a character to ever-more bizarre—and oftentimes murderous or, at least, criminal—acts. Well-known examples include *Memento*, *Black Swan* and *Session 9*.

Horror Thrillers: Since they both rely so much on tension and anxiety, thrillers and horror films intersect often. Some thrillers are as much or nearly as much horror films as they are thrillers. Examples include *The Silence of the Lambs*, *Halloween* and *Devil*.

Spy Thrillers: These are among the most popular films in the world. Some of the examples are beyond obvious, such as the James Bond 007 franchise. The Jack Ryan and Jason Bourne films are also good examples of this type of film.

Action Thrillers: Thriller storytelling techniques can be very effective at getting the audience to care about the characters, and putting those characters in harm's way is more thrilling for the audience when they do care. *Taken*, *Predator* and *Die Hard* all used thriller elements quite successfully.

Legal Thrillers: This category includes some of the best examples of the form. *A Few Good Men*, *The Firm* and many other films have successfully turned the drudgery of court into a setting for some of the finest and most engaging drama around.

Sci-Fi Thrillers: Science fiction films oftentimes incorporate thriller elements in creative and very distressing ways. Examples include *Blade Runner*, *Alien* and *Inception*.

Erotic Thrillers: These take romance and turn it on its head. *Basic Instinct*, *Jade* and *Wild Things* are all examples.

There are many other subgenres and some of the films listed in later chapters can be categorized in the aforementioned or other subgenres. Thriller elements appear in many different types of films, simply because they embody good storytelling techniques and because they can get the audience involved in the story in meaningful and memorable ways.

Differences with Other Genres

The thriller element can be present or absent in many different genres of film and, moreover, a thriller can be a pure thriller as well. Here are some of the differences between thrillers and movies in three other genres that oftentimes incorporate thriller elements, but that are distinct genres of their own.

Versus Horror

A defining element of the thriller genre makes the contrast between thrillers and horror films easy to understand.

Thrillers are films that, in many cases, rely on the realistic nature of their stories to elicit feelings of dread from their audience. For example, *Se7en* most certainly has elements of horror in it, but the setting is a very believable one: just a rough part of Any City, USA. There is nothing supernatural about the antagonist in the film, either, which makes the whole situation even tenser, since there is really no reason to believe that anything that happens in the film could not happen in real life.

Some horror films start out as thrillers, but change at some point during the story or later in the franchise, if one develops around the movies. *Halloween*, as David Hohl points out, is a thriller through and through, until the final moment where a supernatural element is asserted.

A thriller must be real, because nothing is so frightening as reality. The fantastic elements of pure horror give the audience an escape hatch. Jason Voorhees could never survive the abuse he takes in the *Friday the 13th* films. Freddy Krueger is really kind of a silly villain. Horror films get their results by exposing the audience to the horrific, but those horrors happen in a fantasy world, which lessens the terror, if not the fun.

Kevin Spacey's character in *Se7en* could be your next-door neighbor. In fact, who's saying he's not? Therein lies the difference, to a great extent, between thrillers and horror films.

Note that some films—such as *The Sixth Sense*—combine supernatural elements into the thriller genre, but are not horror thrillers.

Versus Pure Crime

Stories centering on crime oftentimes have thriller elements to them, but they are certainly not all thrillers in and of themselves. Many are procedural, following the protagonist as s/he unravels a crime and owing more to author Sir Arthur Conan Doyle than they do to Hitchcock. Other crime films fit more easily into other categories. *The Godfather*, for example, is a thrilling film to watch, but it is a mob movie more than a thriller.

To be a true crime thriller, the audience must be on the edge of their seats. *Heat*, for example, was rife with tension and put the audience in the uncomfortable position of not knowing whom they should be rooting for. The fact that the film drew from elements of real bank robberies made it even more riveting.

To be a crime thriller, a film must grip the audience in an uncommon way and the result must be tension, fear, dread and other like feelings. A crime thriller doesn't make you want to be the cop or the robber; it makes you fear for both of them.

Versus Pure Action

Thriller films oftentimes have incredible action sequences in them that only add to the tension. Examples include the aforementioned *Taken* and *A History of Violence*. The reason that the action in these films is so engaging, particularly compared to the violence one usually sees in action movies is, again, because it is depicted as being part of the real world.

Some action thrillers incorporate other genres, as well. For instance, *The Dark Knight* certainly was effective in raising anxiety levels, but was also a superhero/comic book movie.

The Professional is another film that successfully combines action elements—shootouts, elite killers, assassinations—into a thriller film.

In some cases, thriller films are a lot like action films, but more grown-up. The characters are in real danger, the violence has very real—and very nasty—consequences and the audience feels the tension throughout. In action films, the effect is more like that of a rollercoaster. There are thrills, but one is aware that they are never really in danger of things going off the rails.

A thriller, no matter what subgenre it might fit in—if any—always makes you feel like the danger is real, every wonderful second of it.

Chapter 2:

Beyond Genres: What Makes a Thriller Work?

Thrillers, because they can cross over into other genres, oftentimes incorporate elements of those other genres to find their winning formula. For instance, a thriller that crosses over into the horror genre will oftentimes incorporate the same impenetrable blacks at the edges of the screen, haunting music and sudden scares that you'd expect in horror films. A thriller that crosses over into action, such as *Taken*, will incorporate a lot of dark, moody and tense scenes with sudden explosions of action that put most pure action films to shame.

Thrillers thrive on combining elements of other genres from which they borrow with the unique elements that make a thriller film what it is. When they're done right, the effect is incredible and, quite often, it serves to take what would be cheap horror movie jump-scare mongering or dunderheaded action and elevate it to the level of very adult, engaging storytelling.

What makes a thriller work, however, can be understood in terms of some conventions that tend to work repeatedly. Oftentimes, a thriller takes a regular setting, adds a dark twist here and there and adds characters to the mix that create a sense of foreboding at every turn, even when the most mundane action is taking place on the screen.

Setting

Figure 1: The Bates Motel.

The thriller genre is among the most diverse of film genres where setting is concerned. They sometimes utilize settings as characters that have relevance to the story. For instance, the hyper-advanced villain lairs in James Bond movies usually figure heavily into the climax of the films and, in some cases, are nearly characters in and of themselves. In other cases, the settings are about mood more than scenery. The film *Se7en*, with its perpetual rain and hideously ugly and ubiquitous signs of urban decay, uses the scenery to reflect the essence of the story itself, which is a dark and dangerous place, to be sure. No one in their right mind would want to check into the Bates Motel, and the imposing architecture of the home looming over the bland hotel itself rather implies the darkness lurking behind the bland front that Norman Bates shows to visitors.

Thriller films tend to succeed or fail based on how many reversals they can hand the audience without making it all so unrealistic that the audience becomes disengaged. Setting can play into that. John Doe, the killer from *Se7en*, would be wholly unbelievable were he to show up in Beaver Cleaver's neighborhood, but cast him in a murky, filthy and polluted urban environment and he's suddenly believable; a reflection of the filth, cruelty and unforgiving nature of the city he calls home.

Whenever you do sit down to watch a thriller, be aware that you'll understand the film much better if you do consider the setting. Sometimes you'll really be looking at what amounts to a Russian nesting doll where the scenery is concerned. For example, in *Magic*, Corky battles it out with his darker half—embodied in the nightmare fuel that is his dummy, Fats—in an unassuming cabin, where he's trying to get away from it all. The character is hiding in a bland space in the same way that the awful darkness he carries within himself is hiding under his bland and actually quite wimpy surface personality.

Sometimes, when you open the door to the most banal-seeming spaces, the horrors you find are far beyond what you could have imagined, and good thriller writers and directors are masters of getting you to open that door, peek inside and find out that, sometimes, things are much, much worse than you could have ever suspected.

Infinite Variety, Unending Suspense

Settings in thriller films speak to the tremendous diversity of this genre. They also speak to how much freedom the writers of thrillers have to explore in terms of where the action takes place. James Bond may find himself in the most glamorous casino in the world one moment, in a gritty, third-world cityscape the next and underwater battling it out with elite terrorist goon squads by the time evening rolls around. There's really no limit to where a thriller might take the audience in telling its story and that is one of the elements that make this genre so very powerful.

Of course, you don't want to head off to the most exotic, frightening or intriguing destinations in the world without a good tour guide. Quite often, the audience discovers the environment and the people within it along with the protagonist. Oftentimes, that means that the tour guide is the villain.

Thrillers are among the most prolific film genres of all where creating truly memorable villains is concerned, and exploring those villains and what motivates them is part and parcel of understanding and appreciating the genre on the whole.

The Players

Thrillers succeed when the story behind them is told well. It's hard to imagine a thriller without a villain who is just as compelling as the hero, though they are not always so substantial. When they are, however, they oftentimes serve to move the plot forward more than the protagonist does and, in some cases, the audience may even find themselves secretly wishing the villain would get away with their crimes, simply because such interesting characters do lend so much to the world in which we live, even if they're only imaginary.

The protagonist in thriller films tends to be very tough, though, again, this is not always the case. Bryan Mills of *Taken* and Jason Bourne of the *Bourne* films are certainly not to be trifled with. On the other hand, Dan Gallagher, the protagonist of *Fatal Attraction,* is terrorized by his jilted paramour, a woman that Bourne or Mills would have likely made disappear without a trace.

Quite often, the deadliest protagonist characters have a moral compass that allows us to empathize with them, even as they're killing off compelling villains. Villains who are real human beings, presumably with families, friends and maybe even pets.

Conversely, some of the weakest characters have a lack of strength that goes right down to the core of them and we're asked to overlook their weakness. If Dan Gallagher could have found the strength to be true to his wife and family, his path would have never crossed that of an obsessive psychopath. Interestingly, it's easy enough to sympathize with Alex Forrest, the bunny-boiling villain of *Fatal*

Attraction, as her psychopathy is an entirely separate issue from Dan's moral spinelessness.

Let's get started by taking a look at thriller film villains and what makes them tick.

Chapter 3:

The Villain

Thrillers are great places to look if you want to enjoy some of the greatest movie villains ever created. In the best cases, they represent creative and clever twists on the villain as a general character type, but they can usually be understood as belonging to various archetypes. Here are some of the most famous.

The Sympathetic Villain

Many villains in thrillers are sympathetic in certain regards. Norman Bates, after all, was insane and in desperate need of treatment of some sort. It wasn't evil that led him to kill; it was his detachment from reality. Anything from abuse to PTSD to a brain injury or tumor can cause behavior similarly murderous to Bates' from any human being. You may fear him, he may haunt your dreams from time to time, but it's not his fault that he's as crazy as he is.

Sympathetic villains are not anti-heroes. Anti-heroes exist to allow use to indulge our outlaw fantasies and, most of the time, anti-heroes are characters that go against authority or social conventions to some ultimately laudable end. Sympathetic villains are villainous through and through. They just make it hard not to like them and, sometimes, they make it very hard to root for the hero, which is part of the fun of thriller films in general.

Alex Forrest, again, is a great example of a sympathetic villain. While Forrest relentlessly chips away at the audience's ability to feel sympathy for her with her increasingly bizarre and violent behavior, there is something comprehensible in her actions. She was fragile to begin with and a character that plays her—attorneys are great characters whenever a writer wants to convey that someone is, at heart, a liar—finally pushes her over the edge. She doesn't want to be ignored; she doesn't want to be used. Any audience member, though they may be horrified by Alex's actions, can sympathize with those feelings and feel a sort of revulsion at the way that Gallagher treated her. Alex didn't need to be shot to death. She needed someone to understand her and to help her with her obsessive nature. What she got was jilted, ignored, dismissed, half-drowned and a chest full of gunshot wounds. Is she really the villain here?

Thrillers aren't afraid of these kinds of reversals, which helps keep them free of the cardboard villains oftentimes seen in horror and action films.

The Secret Society
Sometimes, the most deliciously wicked schemes are launched by organizations rather than individuals. In *The Skulls*, for instance, a secret organization of wealthy and connected Ivy League students is the villain. Would any of them be individually capable of the evil that their secret organization perpetrates? Perhaps, but bringing together a bunch of morally flawed characters with vast notions of entitlement almost always seems to make the sum worse than its parts.

The secret society tends to be a bit different than the criminal syndicate, described below. The secret society is often more obscure in its aims and its motivations than a syndicate. A syndicate tends to be about getting money and power through crime, but doesn't seek to outright overthrow the existing structure. SPECTRE—the Special

Executive for Counter-intelligence, Terrorism, Revenge and Extortion—was long James Bond's nemesis throughout the franchise. This organization was not one made up of mere criminals, they were connected, powerful and quite brilliant individuals who commanded the resources of a private army, complete with secret lairs, submarines and more. They were a genuine threat to the existing order, and they meant to be.

The Da Vinci Code has religious authorities as its conspirators. *Jacob's Ladder* has government conspiracy at the heart of its plot, a reveal not given away fully until the end.

Secret societies can work very well as thriller villains. They are oftentimes possessed of knowledge far beyond what the audience or protagonist possesses. In the case of spy thriller secret societies, the societies are fascinating because of the implication that they function nearly as governments in and of themselves, except that they usually exist to subvert modern governments and to establish empires of pure law and evil, something that will be discussed shortly.

Additionally, while syndicates are quite often made up of people who are trying to stay ahead of the law, secret societies are often beyond it or even in control of it. The various corrupt officials in *L.A. Confidential*, for instance, may be powerful enough to intimidate the average person, but it's hard to believe that Blofeld from SPECTRE would really find any of them to be more than petty criminals.

The Syndicate
Where societies such as SPECTRE are secret, syndicates are merely exclusive. You have to be a criminal to belong to one and, most often, you have to hold the interests of the syndicate above all else. At least, insofar as that is possible in an organization made up of self-motivated, lawless individuals.

In the film *Heat*, for instance, the syndicate may be a small group of bank robbers, but they are all good enough at what they do and motivated enough to constitute as much of a threat as any large mob outfit. They are all somewhat loyal to one another, but only so far as their individual senses of self-motivation allow. These are not good guys, but they do stick together and help one another enough to achieve the group's goals, the hallmark of a syndicate.

Films such as *The Departed* play on a common trope with thrillers, allowing us to see a criminal syndicate that most people would normally regard as a threat as being under threat itself by law enforcement. This can ratchet up the tension quite a bit and sometimes make it difficult for the audience to determine whose side they're really on, given that the syndicates sometimes have more familial and sympathetic motivations for sticking together than do the law enforcement agencies that are oftentimes the protagonist organizations in the film.

Sometimes, the syndicates are just pure evil. The human traffickers in *Taken*, for instance, are about as bad as they come, and they pay for it dearly.

The Madman

The madman comes in many varieties. Oftentimes, he is a species of killer, such as John Doe in *Se7en*. In other cases, however, the madman is actually not a villain at all. For example, De Niro is certainly mad as a hatter in *Taxi Driver*, but he's also the protagonist of the film.

As is the case in real life, madness in thriller films is often a complex affair. Some madmen are simple sharks in the water, such as Norman Bates. Others are much more complex, such as Hannibal Lecter. They may advance the plot and even help the protagonist, in some cases. Madmen may also provide the foil for the protagonist, showing how the protagonist, despite their own flaws, is more relatable as a human being in light of the lunacy that the madman— or madwoman—represents.

Max Cady from *Cape Fear* is a good example of madness as it is oftentimes portrayed in thriller films. He's violent, sociopathic and motivated to get revenge to the point where it doesn't take a Ph.D. to diagnose the man as insane. Nonetheless, there is a reason behind why he so badly wants revenge and that makes him easier to understand. In horror films, madness sometimes exists in a vacuum. The family in *The Texas Chainsaw Massacre* is completely mad and the audience can accept that. In thriller films, the madman or madwoman often has a triggering moment in their past, allowing the story to retain the element of realism that is so vital for a thriller to succeed. Perhaps the audience is glad that they never crossed paths with Max Cady but, at the same time, the reasons behind his fury become understandable enough once the plot starts to unfold.

The Brute

The brute is just that. These characters are all force and frequently they're not the main villain in a thriller film, but serve to move the story forward by giving the hero a challenge to get through before they ultimately reach the level or architect of a conspiracy. There are cases, however, when the antagonist is simply a brute. Frank Booth of *Blue Velvet* is a madman, to be sure. He's completely consumed by his passions, is utterly and completely violent and is wholly unpredictable. In those qualities, he is also very much a brute.

Where the brute figures into many thrillers—particularly spy and crime thrillers—is as a henchman. Jaws from the *James Bond* series is a particularly well-known example of this. So is Oddjob, from *Goldfinger*. These characters oftentimes provide an important element of peril in films where the protagonist is particularly gifted at violence, such as *Taken*, the Jason Bourne films and the *007* series.

Oddjob serves as a great example of this. James Bond is up against Auric Goldfinger, a genius by any measure, thoroughly corrupt and possessed of tremendous resources. James Bond is tasked with outwitting this accomplished and powerful villain.

While Goldfinger provides a frustrating and deadly challenge for the secret agent, he isn't an adequate foil in regards to bringing out what makes James Bond an interesting character in and of himself. Bond is not only cultured, suave and sophisticated, he's also a character who is remarkably deadly physically, and that needs to be established. The fight with Oddjob provides the proof of Bond's deadliness.

The brute oftentimes has to push the hero to the hero's limits. In one of the most tense scenes in *Taken*, Bryan Mills takes on a thug who is nearly his equal in hand-to-hand combat. Mills, in fact, nearly loses the fight with this man, but ultimately prevails. This brute not only functions to demonstrate that the syndicate that kidnapped Mills' daughter is indeed a group of experienced and skilled killers; he also functions to establish that the 'skills' that Mills has make him the deadliest threat of all.

When watching thrillers, one does well to remember that the brute isn't just a 'boss fight', as gamers call it, for the protagonist. Brutes oftentimes serve to prove how dangerous the protagonist really is and how much trouble the antagonist has coming their way. Watch Mills take out a very tough and dangerous henchman without showing a hint of emotion and it's easier to believe it when he takes out a pack of them in the film's climactic scene.

Evil Incarnate

Evil incarnate sometimes pops up in thriller films, though it's most often seen in those films that tend to overlap with horror. It can, however, rear its ugly head and when it does, it's quite effective.

This is well explained by the trope Card Carrying Villainy as explained on TVTropes. Evil incarnate describes a villain who really just exists to be evil. As the site points out, they oftentimes want to corrupt good people, to control good people—or conquer the world, as the cliché goes—or they simply want to destroy everything and anything they come across. Some men just want to watch the world burn, as *The Dark Knight* taught us.

Evil incarnate can come in different flavors, which are detailed further along in the book. The thing to watch for in a villain who is simply evil is the absence of another motivating factor. For instance, in *A View to a Kill*, Max Zorin, the villain, is the result of Nazi genetic experimentation. The children that came out of this experimentation were psychopathic, but Zorin is so cold and calculating that he can only be described as evil. His psychopathy just makes him better at it, but he's evil through and through and the audience is made well aware of it.

Where pure evil in thrillers is concerned, it's important to differentiate it from pure evil in horror. Michael Myers of the *Halloween* franchise, for instance, is specifically understood to be an incarnation of pure evil, which is why he's unkillable. He's supernatural to the core. Conversely, evil characters in thrillers often embody a realistic type of evil. One that is cold, calculating, efficient, and ruthless above all, but one that is killable and subject to the same human weaknesses that anyone else is subject to. The evil you'll find in a thriller movie is usually not far off from the evil you'll see human beings exhibit toward one another in everyday life, which is what makes thriller evil ultimately more frightening than horror evil.

The Darker Half

This is one of the most effective tropes in thriller films in general. It allows the writers to set up the reversal, which leaves the audience aghast and engages them like nothing else.

In order for the darker half to work, it cannot be a total surprise. Norman Bates, for instance, is shown to have less than perfect control over his emotions early on in the movie, which makes it more believable when the awful truth is revealed.

This trope can function on a relatively understandable level. For instance, Bryan Mills goes absolutely homicidal when his daughter is kidnapped and anyone can understand—and admire—that. His darker half is really just a heroic expression of the capacity for violence. When another Mills, Brad Pitt's character in *Se7en*, executes John Doe in cold blood, the audience sympathizes and understands why. Mills' darker half was, again, triggered by violence against his family and the target of his violence, by any rational if not exactly legal interpretation of morality, had it coming.

Sometimes, however, the darker half is pure terror. Annie Wilkes in *Misery* is a prime example. Little by little, what's terrifying about her creeps to the surface, and the protagonist isn't able to go anywhere to get out of its path or to defend himself, for the most part. This makes her doubly terrifying. She's unpredictable, volatile, violent and dominating, but she's also capable of covering it up with a completely unrevealing exterior. No one knows just how insane she really is.

This Jekyll-and-Hyde setup is one of the most effective for thriller movies. Sometimes, you don't know exactly how dark the main character is, as is the case in *Memento*. In others, you may not even see the evil right there in front of you, such as in *The Usual Suspects*, given that you're dealing with a villain who is a master of their craft and who can cover up every inch of darkness. Most dangerously of all, the villain can do it in a way that would make most people drop their guards utterly.

In other cases, the darkness within is apparent to the audience, but not to the players in the movie. *Magic*, which acquaints the audience very well with the blacker-than-black evil that lurks within Corky's shattered psyche, does so at the expense of the characters that surround him, who may suspect that something is wrong, but who find out far too late in all cases.

Part of what makes thrillers effective is that they have a core of realism to them. This darker half trope is one of the most effective of all for that reason. Stories that invoke it can make the audience feel empowered as they watch an ex-CIA agent demonstrate a terrifying capacity for violence. They can also make the audience cringe in fear, realizing that the nice woman who likes the author's books is completely nuts, obsessive and dangerous in the extreme, and you just try getting away from her.

Classy, Cultured and Pure Evil

Of all the evil tropes in thrillers, this may well be the one that is the most fun for the audience. This villain type is someone we'd all like to know. Sure, they're evil or just dangerous, but they're not really bad people, at least in some regards. Sometimes, it's their intelligence and refinement that makes them attractive. In other cases, it's their sense of morality or fair play, however twisted, that manages to be interesting and attractive to the audience.

In the end, what matters is that you like them somehow, and that makes them a lot of fun to watch, even if they are making the protagonist's life difficult.

Catherine Tramell of *Basic Instinct* is a prime example of this type of villain. She is highly educated and incredibly intelligent. She's also a classic femme fatale in that her sexual charms can lead those around her to ruin, a fact of which she is well aware and that she doesn't mind using to her advantage. Nonetheless, provided one didn't cross her or become too intimately involved with Tramell, she'd probably be a very interesting person to go out for coffee with. She's witty, collected and demonstrates a very respectable ability to get through life getting exactly what she wants along the way. Oftentimes, in movie climaxes where someone is being terrorized by an insane killer, the victim starts demanding to know why the killer is doing what they're doing. Villains like Tramell could probably explain it to those victims in very certain terms and, worse yet, terms that the victims themselves may even understand at some level.

Hannibal Lecter of *Silence of the Lambs* fame provides another fine example of this type of evil. He is a horrible, wicked and thoroughly evil man, but he's also witty, cunning and quite capable. He is someone that the audience can like because of his complexity. Like all real human beings, he has many sides to his personality and, though the frightening ones are something beyond horrific, he also seems like an amusing fellow to spend an evening with; a man with a great understanding of human nature.

Lecter also understands evil at a professorial level. This makes him even more intriguing to the audience, as he can serve as something of a guide through the darkest parts of the human psyche. You may even believe that Hannibal Lecter wouldn't add you to his list of victims, provided you weren't rude and didn't play the flute poorly. Perhaps it would be fun to invite him over for dinner, except…

The classy villain is a great thriller convention. It can be seen throughout the various thriller subgenres. The villains in crime thrillers often have the trappings of an upper-class lifestyle and flaunt it at every occasion. The villains in horror thrillers occasionally balance out their evil tendencies with a very charming and polite personality that serves to make them even more dangerous.

Chapter 4

Know Thy Enemy: Evil Tropes in Thrillers

Villains can provide an embodiment of evil, but they are not always evil itself. In thriller movies, evil is sometimes understandable because there is a very human motivation behind it—greed, for example. In other cases, it's harder to understand, particularly when the character perpetrating various acts of evil is so thoroughly corrupt or insane that's it's difficult for a normal person to relate to them at all.

Evil, however, does have conventions that make it more comprehensible, at least in fictional portrayals. Where thrillers are concerned, it is evil in action that is the subject of study. While moral or ethical evil may be behind it, the actions of a villain can be understood as evil put into practice. How that evil is put into practice can reveal a great deal about the villain and what motivates them and, ultimately, what kind of evil they happen to be.

There is a sort of evil that is technically not evil. This is neutrality in the face of evil. It plays to the concept that all one needs to do to be evil is to permit evil to happen unopposed. This is oftentimes one of the most challenging things to watch for the audience. Sometimes, when a character doesn't intervene to prevent evil, it's easy enough to understand why they wouldn't, given that the circumstances are oftentimes made deliberately terrifying for effect.

Whatever name you call it by, thrillers serve up plenty of evil and, like all complex dishes, there are some variations that one must understand before they can appreciate what they're indulging in.

Coldly Neutral
While there is no shortage of literature and no shortage of movies that discuss the terror of looking into the face of evil, sometimes looking into the face of indifference is a far more terrifying thing. Some of the most effective thriller villains aren't so much evil as they are utterly detached from the consequences of their actions and the effect that they have on others.

In thriller films, one popular way to characterize a villain is to create a character that is so utterly heartless, devoid of emotion and, at the same time, consumed with a particular purpose that they embody an entirely other form of terror. This isn't the villain that chases you through the night, taunting you, completely consumed by their own rage. This isn't the villain that is compelled to destroy the world and everyone in it. The coldly neutral villain is a villain who simply does not care. They are the villain who has a purpose to their existence—or not—and who is simply unaware of the suffering they bring to others' lives, if they are aware that other beings have feelings at all.

The Psychopath
The psychopath is, particularly in horror movies, oftentimes cast as someone who is wildly dangerous, chaotic and thoroughly wicked. Thriller movies usually take a more accurate approach to the psychopath. *Psychology Today* gives a good overview of what psychopathy really is. One of the elements of their definition that is particularly pertinent to the thriller genre is that psychopathy is

extremely difficult to spot. In thrillers, this can be played up to great effect.

A psychopath can be a volatile character. They can be prone to violent fits of rage, or, in some cases, rage brought about by some sort of a delusion. Not all psychopaths, however, spend their days battling imaginary demons, getting revenge on people long dead, stalking innocent people in showers and so forth. A prime example of this can be found in the 2000 film *American Psycho*.

In the film, Patrick Bateman gives one of the best first-person descriptions of what it is to be a psychopath. It speaks to the character's detachment from his emotions and, more importantly, it describes his utter detachment from the people around him:

> *"There is an idea of a Patrick Bateman; some kind of abstraction. But there is no real me: only an entity, something illusory. And though I can hide my cold gaze, and you can shake my hand and feel flesh gripping yours and maybe you can even sense our lifestyles are probably comparable... I simply am not there."*

Most human beings have an identity that is partially defined socially and partially defined internally. For the psychopath character, there is no identity. There is only an emotionless sort of existence broken up by occasional explosions of hatred, violence, wrath or other similar emotions.

In her *Writer's Guide to Character Traits* by Linda N Edelstein, Ph.D., the author gives an overview of some of the traits of a psychopath. One of the primary things that define a psychopath is the lack of control over behaviors that other people would understand to be wrong. As the book states, a psychopath has no conscience.

Because he is such a great example of a thriller film psychopath, looking at some of the character traits of a classic psychopath and comparing them to the Patrick Bateman character is useful to understanding how these characters are typically established and developed in thriller films.

According to Edelstein, a psychopath feels alienated from other people, something the above quote clearly demonstrates in the case of Bateman. A psychopath is typically charming and, again, the above quote is useful. You can shake his hand and sense that your lifestyles are probably comparable. You feel that you can relate to this person but, underneath the surface, they feel utterly nothing for you, nor do they feel anything for anyone else they come into contact with.

Psychopaths tend to be motivated by money, they tend to have no strong feelings one way or the other on any given subject, they become bored easily and, when they do become bored, the ways they find to amuse themselves can be downright horrific.

One of the final traits that the book points out about psychopaths that is particularly relevant to thriller films is that they tend to have a complete disregard for the rights of others. A psychopath is among the most coldly neutral characters imaginable. They are not evil, as being evil would—twisted as it may be—entail embracing a philosophy and having a particular opinion about something. A psychopath doesn't function in that way.

It is important to realize that not all psychopaths are equally given over to their disorders. As an example of this, in television, the title character from the *Dexter* series goes through a transformation throughout the story that winds up with him exhibiting far more human compassion than a psychopath would normally be expected to understand. Just as not all people who suffer from depression are equally depressed, not all people who suffer from psychopathy are equally psychopathic.

One other element of psychopathy that's important to point out is that it doesn't necessarily entail any detachment from reality. In fact, your average psychopath can be just as connected to reality as any other human being. Psychosis is a separate mental condition, characterized by being detached from reality. A psychopath is often not only fully cognizant of the difference between the world around them and their own imaginings, they are typically incredibly efficient, ruthless and successful types who have no problem advancing themselves at the expense of others. In thriller films, this makes them ideal hitmen, femme fatales and other antagonistic characters.

The Sociopath

Sociopathy is generally diagnosed using the same criteria that are used for psychopathy. In fact, for all intents and purposes, they are so similar that the differences would really only be relevant to someone working in a clinical setting.

A sociopath, like a psychopath, feels no compassion or empathy for any of the people that they share their lives with. They use people freely, discard them when unneeded and, as a *Psychology Today* article entitled "Understanding the Sociopath" makes clear, they oftentimes emotionally destroy everybody around them. Sociopaths often cover up a great deal of anger with a very placid exterior and, when that anger explodes, the consequences of it can be devastating for anybody who happens to be in the path of the sociopath.

Psychopathy, Sociopathy and Moral Weakness

In some films, the protagonist will actually be a character who exhibits either psychopathic or sociopathic tendencies. For example, in the film *Fatal Attraction,* Dan Gallagher exhibits what could be construed as some rather sociopathic behavior. Principally, without any regard to the consequences of his actions, he initiates an affair with Alex Forrest. Not being a true sociopath, he does feel regretful for it, but he also winds up hurting Alex so significantly that it shatters her fragile psyche, setting into motion the horrible events that follow.

A psychopath and a sociopath both share a complete detachment from a sense of right and wrong in the moral sense. Either of these types of personalities, for instance, could be characterized as a sleazy investment advisor who deliberately steers you into bad investments because it benefits them and then simply fails to understand why you would even be upset about that. It's not that they don't understand why they're not able to get away with it; it's that they genuinely do not understand why people have emotions and why they, as they generally do harbor some sense of narcissism, should be bothered to deal with the feelings and emotions of other people, even if it is the actions of the sociopath or psychopath themselves that give rise to those emotions in the people that they hurt.

The Mastermind

The mastermind is one of the most compelling types of villains out there. The Villains Wiki gives a rather serviceable definition of this type of a villain.

The mastermind is a villain who plans everything out to an incredible degree of detail. They may be psychopaths and they may be sociopaths, but they may also be completely, though coldly, sane. What makes them truly neutral as far as villains go is that they are really only dedicated to whatever plan it is they have in mind.

Keyser Soze of *The Usual Suspects* is probably one of the best examples of the mastermind in thriller movies. He is obviously a psychopath, as well. This man has absolutely no regard for the lives of anyone he comes into contact with, including his own family, as the movie reveals. He is calculating, cold, ruthless and, in fact, such a fine example of a criminal mastermind that other criminals fear him and regard him as something of a legend.

It's also notable how well the Soze character manages to lie to avoid being taken into custody. There is absolutely nothing that the detectives interviewing him could take as a 'tell', as poker players call it. The man is completely devoid of the standard range of human emotions and, therefore, he is fully capable of lying without having any of the telling reactions that people tend to demonstrate due to their being uncomfortable— again, at the moral level—with telling someone something that isn't true.

Silence of the Lambs also gave the world one of its finest examples of a mastermind-type villain in Hannibal Lecter. Even under an incredibly high level of security, this character manages to engineer an escape plan and carry it through with incredible efficiency and effectiveness. He is always at least one step ahead of you and, in fact, probably far more than one step ahead. Just when you feel that you may have caught him at his game, you find out that you're the one being played.

The reason that this type of villain is so very effective in thriller movies is only revealed when the writing is good. The mastermind has to have a plan that is, with very little suspension of disbelief, plausible. It has to seem like their plan would actually work. The plan is oftentimes revealed in retrospect, and the audience must believe that the villain could actually get away with it.

This, once again, does serve as a good example of how horror movies and thriller movies differ. It's easy to believe that Michael Myers can catch up to you when you're running at a full sprint and he's walking at a rather casual pace, simply because he is pure evil and he doesn't really need a realistic way to deal with this issue. In the case of Hannibal Lecter, however, the reason you believe that he could actually slip out of police custody and catch up to the man who tormented Lecter while Lecter was in prison is because, given the portrayal of the character and his backstory, it is entirely believable that he would skin a human being alive, calmly conceal himself within that person's skin and make his escape.

Of course, the mastermind—Lecter, in this case— doesn't do this in the service of evil or to disrupt law and order; he does it because it benefits him. He is a psychopath and a coldly neutral one at that.

A Framework for Understanding: Beliefs and Behaviors

Because so many thriller films do deal with violence, it is useful to put into play some of the tools that are used to understand violence in real life. In the book *Facing Violence: Preparing for the Unexpected*, author Rory Miller gives an excellent model that can be used to understand how some of the villains in thriller movies differ from other people.

The author references a hierarchical understanding of beliefs and actions that include beliefs at the lowest level, values at the next highest level, morals at the third level and ethics at the very highest level. It is the moral level, or lack thereof, that separates the psychopath and the sociopath from the normal person.

Beliefs are those things that all of us just believe. They include things such as believing that stealing is acceptable or unacceptable. Values demonstrate how you respond to your belief in action. For instance, you may believe that theft is wrong but, if a child were starving during a famine, you may very well steal a loaf of bread to feed that child, reckoning that your belief in compassion outweighs your belief that theft is wrong.

Morals are the next level. Morals simply describe things that you instinctively believe are right or wrong, even though they may not trace directly back to your values or your beliefs. For example, punching someone because you're angry with them—for most people—just feels wrong. You could go on a long speech about why you believe it's wrong, how you believe that it's wrong because it's against the law and therefore you opt not to take that path or whatever else, but it just *feels* wrong at a certain level.

A psychopath or a sociopath doesn't have this moral sense. This is what makes them so effective in thrillers. They cross boundaries that endanger or simply inconvenience the protagonists, but they also allow us, who exist in a way that is largely defined by our sense of morality and right and wrong, to experience a little bit of the dark side in a safe way. After all, while no normal human being would ever think of committing his crimes, everybody can, in some dark place that they normally keep hidden, probably relate to the type of rage that Patrick Bateman feels and, at times, the sense of detachment he feels from others as well.

Wickedly Evil

A good thriller movie is usually centered on characters that seem very human. Being that these characters are oftentimes quite complex, they typically evolve throughout the story and, because of that, it can be very difficult to label any character—even a villain—as good or evil.

It's also useful to point out that the definition of evil is something that philosophers have debated for literally thousands of years. Is evil immorality or amorality? Is evil a thing in and of itself or is it simply the absence of the good that some philosophers believe naturally exists in the human heart? Is evil a goal toward which someone can work or does it merely entail erasing all of the good from the world?

In a thriller film, evil will often be defined by action rather than philosophy. Theological and philosophical arguments aside, an evil character usually takes actions that a normal—or good—character would find morally repugnant. In the simplest terms, the difference between a character who is genuinely evil and one who is coldly neutral is that the wicked actions an evil character takes are oftentimes things that are, in and of themselves, goals. Because of this, and because thrillers tend to stray from the blocky definitions of good and evil that are popular in a great deal of storytelling, evil is actually a trope more commonly observed in horror films than in thriller films. Nonetheless, a little evil here and there does a thriller film good and, in fact, some of the most memorable and—dare one say it?—lovable villains are actually quite evil.

Categorizing Evil

The following system for understanding the nature of evil actually comes from the world of roleplaying games, specifically Dungeons & Dragons. In such games, players create characters that, through a combination of live-action roleplaying and dice-rolling, live out their fictional lives, much in the same way that characters in stories each live out a fictional life.

This categorization scheme utilizes two axes. The first is good, neutral and evil. The second is law, neutral and chaos. Given that villains who aren't neutral are typically evil—though there are exceptions to this rule—one need only look to whether or not they have some sort of code of personal ethics or honor or adherence to the law that they observe; have an utter indifference to law and order or chaos; or whether they actively seek to promote chaos and entropy at every turn to determine what type of evil one is dealing with. It can be eminently useful for gaining a deeper understanding of some of the villains in thriller films.

Lawful Evil
Upholding the law doesn't necessarily mean upholding any sort of a sense of decency. For a great example of this, one needs look no further than John Doe in *Se7en*. This character, perhaps better than most thriller villains, demonstrates what lawful evil truly is.

John Doe is committing his horrific crimes because he is following what he believes to be an absolute authority: biblical law. Each of his victims is guilty—in his mind—of breaking the law in that they have committed one of the seven deadly sins. Each of his punishments for breaking those laws is ironic, such as one of his victims being force-fed to death in punishment for being a glutton.

What makes John Doe lawful evil is that all of his crimes have to conform to his idea of what is acceptable and unacceptable under a divine law. Each of his victims somehow has to embody breaking the law and committing one of the seven deadly sins. To his mind, it is breaking these laws that makes each of these people deserving of the horrible deaths that they endure. Whether or not he gains pleasure from it—and it most certainly seems that he does—is irrelevant to the fact that they have all broken what he believes to be the most important of all laws.

John Doe, interestingly, can also be seen as embodying the crusader character type, which is a character who believes that they are doing good and is so blinded to the extreme nature of their actions in the pursuit of good that they end up being essentially evil. John Doe believes that he is doing what is right, but what he is doing is so very wrong and so unnecessarily cruel that there is absolutely no way that anyone but John Doe himself could see his actions as anything but evil.

The most obvious examples of lawful evil characters are characters that belong to some sort of corrupt authority structure, such as Nazis during the Second World War. Drawing from this common portrayal of lawful evil is the aforementioned SPECTRE organization used as the antagonist in many James Bond films. This organization is structured to the point that its members are often known by numbers rather than names and, if one should fail in their duties, punishment is generally swift and merciless.

Neutral (Pure) Evil

Purely evil characters can be described as neutral evil. To use a variation on a popular Internet expression, they are only in it for the evil. They don't care whether or not there is some sort of guiding—though corrupted—structure in place that condones their evil actions, unless that structure is necessary for their own benefit. Likewise, if burning down the system will further their own ends, a neutral evil character will be filling up a gas can and buying matches in short order.

Bad Lieutenant, a crime thriller, gives a great example of this sort of evil in the main character of the story. He is a police lieutenant, as the name implies, and he will use his legal authority at any point and in any way he can to benefit himself. He will just as easily engage in crime, if he finds there is some benefit in it for him. His actions are violent, merciless, self-motivated and oftentimes involve him enjoying the same indulgences for which he has also presumably arrested people.

Detective Alonzo Harris in the film *Training Day* could also be seen as embodying this type of evil. Whether he works within a system or without, it makes little difference. His primary motivation is getting what he wants and, if necessary, taking it from other people.

The human traffickers in *Taken* can also be understood to embody this sort of evil. They have a structure within which they work, given that their organization has a definite hierarchy and, in fact, the protagonist working his way up that hierarchy is one of the sources of tension that the writers use to keep this particular film moving forward. While the criminals do work within a structure and their business is obviously based on making and honoring contracts, they also subvert the law in that, of course, human trafficking is illegal. If a structure benefits them, they employ it. If a structure hinders them, they subvert it.

Chaotic Evil

Chaotic evil is the type of evil that not only is exploitative, cruel and capricious, but that also delights in destroying any authority structure it comes across and doing so in a way that harms the greatest number of people possible or, at the very least, harms someone in a particularly horrific way.

Skyfall, part of the James Bond franchise, has a villain who is a particularly illustrative incarnation of this type of evil. Silva, the villain, wants to utterly destroy the MI6 organization and to kill most anyone involved with it. Silva sees it as an entirely corrupt organization that he wants to destroy through any means necessary. He seems to prefer accomplishing this goal with as much murder and chaos as possible.

The film *Patriot Games* features as its antagonist organization a group that is splintered off from the IRA. This organization engages in various terrorist activities, primarily to discredit the actual IRA, which fits the bill as far as being evil and wanting to take down an existing power structure, even if that power structure happens to be one that has engaged in terrorism itself.

Barring criminals that seek specifically to join up with organizations, chaotic evil is likely most any criminal's natural alignment. They obviously have little regard for the law and, in fact, most criminals will seek to subvert it—if not outright overthrow it—at any opportunity. The evil element of their personality is that element that finds joy in harming, tormenting or otherwise ruining the lives of the people who the villains encounter, particularly those people who happen to inconvenience them in some way.

It's important to understand that chaotic evil is not insane. Someone who is insane—not by the clinical definition, but by the definition usually employed by thriller writers—is generally random in their actions. A truly chaotic evil character doesn't necessarily despise organization of any sort, particularly if that organization helps them to further their own ends. They do, however, tend to despise it to the point of wanting to destroy any organization that limits their ability to profit or to indulge their own hedonistic impulses. What makes them evil is that, more than from anything else, they gain pleasure from the suffering of others.

Barking Mad
A character that has truly crossed the line and become insane is oftentimes one that is confused with a character who is evil. In the context of thriller movies, the difference is important to understand, as this difference is often what dictates the exact flavor of the tension.

Norman Bates is probably the most well-known example of a thriller character that is completely insane. Murder, obviously, is something that is generally defined as evil, but in the context of a mind as disordered as the one Norman Bates possesses, the entire concept of evil rather falls apart. He commits murders because he has a personality that is utterly disassociated from reality. He is not truly evil. In fact, rather than being victims of an evil tormentor, the victims of Norman Bates are really people who fell prey to someone who was, themselves, tormented.

M, likewise, features a murderer who suffers from a very common feature of severe personality disorders: he hears voices.

The 2003 film *Identity* uses a common insanity theme found in thriller films. The plot revolves around multiple personalities and, while the popular understanding of multiple personalities is miles away from the psychological reality of it, it always makes for good thriller movie fare.

A character that is insane offers writers quite a bit of freedom, particularly when going for a great plot reversal. Because their actions are inherently unpredictable, writers have an entirely plausible motivation to introduce surprises into the story and, in fact, this sometimes ends up creating some of the most memorable moments in movie history, as epitomized in the film *Psycho*.

http://www.psychologytoday.com/basics/psychopathy

Writer's Guide to Character Traits by Linda N Edelstein, Ph.D.

http://www.psychologytoday.com/blog/insight-is-2020/201304/understanding-the-sociopath-cause-motivation-relationship

http://villains.wikia.com/wiki/Category:Mastermind

Facing Violence: Preparing for the Unexpected Rory Miller

Chapter 5:

The Protagonist

One of the great things about thriller films is that they're not afraid of moral ambiguity. In fact, they thrive on it. The heroes in thriller films can be insane or, in some cases, have a touch of evil to them that makes them more compelling than the average hero.

Perhaps the reason for this is that those characters who have their complexities and, moreover, who aren't exactly knights in shining armor when it comes to those complexities, are more like real people. The protagonists in thriller films can be flawed, scared, outmatched and have serious questions about what they believe to be right and wrong, and still keep the audience engaged.

The protagonists, in fact, sometimes bring about the worst of what happens to them through their own actions, which sets up interesting scenarios where the audience isn't sure who to root for.

Who Wants to Be a Hero?

Consider for a moment what it takes to be a hero. A hero can be described, in some cases, as a person who takes extraordinary actions under extraordinary circumstances. For example, running into a burning building to save somebody who's helpless when you're not a firefighter, don't have firefighting gear and really are just doing so out of genuine concern for another human being would be considered a heroic action. It's not an action that everybody would take and, in fact, most people can be forgiven for not taking such an action, since it could potentially result in the loss of two lives rather than one.

Not every protagonist in a thriller film is actually a hero. Poor Dan Gallagher in *Fatal Attraction,* for example, isn't a hero caught up in a bad situation. He's a man who cheated on his wife with precisely the wrong woman. Jeff Jefferies in *Rear Window,* given his penchant for peeping into other people's houses, is really something of a voyeur.

In *Psycho,* Marion Crane, who so famously dies in the shower, is a thief. She's literally stolen tens of thousands of dollars from one of her employer's customers, but the audience certainly feels for her and, by any stretch of the imagination, she most certainly didn't deserve to die the horrific death she eventually did.

Bryan Mills in *Taken* is also a complex hero. In fact, one could argue that his heroism is only a result of the situation he is in. When not rescuing his daughter from international human traffickers, the man was obviously a hitman of some sort and one can only imagine what sort of political intrigue he was engaged in and how unjust some of his former activities must have been.

Thriller movies are made for grown-ups. Because of that, characters don't need to be drawn in broad strokes, subtlety is certainly within the realm of acceptable writing technique and not every hero needs to be flawless. In fact, in a thriller movie, the fact that the protagonist is often not particularly heroic is precisely what allows the audience to feel for them all the more. Just like every single member of the audience in attendance, the protagonist of the film is a flawed individual who has their own demons to battle.

Because of the complexity of the genre, thriller movies do tend to have some rather interesting characters that serve as heroes. Some of these characters can be broken down into broad types that appear in various movies or that embody some of the traits of the protagonist. Again, because of the complexity involved in thriller writing, most thriller characters do not neatly fit into one category or another, but tend to embody a bit of all of the categories of heroes described below.

The Anti-Hero

The anti-hero is one of the staples of the thriller film. For example, in the 1994 film *The Professional*, the protagonist is a paid killer. Leon, the protagonist, manages to step in and save a young girl from a corrupt group of policemen, but he is still a killer nonetheless. In fact, he starts training the girl to be a killer herself.

What characters like Leon, Bryan Mills and Jason Bourne bring to the table are all of the qualities that would make a villain extremely intimidating in a context that makes them sometimes downright heroic. These aren't 'good guys'. These are people who are, generally, capable of horrific levels of violence and, to some degree, who enjoy that violence. These are masters of killing, stealth, intelligence-gathering and other shady activities. In the right context, however, all of those capacities are things that can be used to serve the ends of people who are being victimized, and in a thriller film this is quite often utilized to create sympathy for the character. In some instances, particularly in films such as *The Professional* and *Taken*, the audience may safely indulge in identifying very strongly with a character that is, essentially, a coldhearted killer, as what that coldhearted killer is doing is, on the whole, a good thing.

The Reformed Criminal

Reformed criminals are sometimes utilized in thriller films in the same way an anti-hero is used. In some cases, however, the reformation of the criminal actually comes during the action in the film. One crime thriller, in particular, provides a great example of this.

In the 1993 film *Killing Zoe*, Zed is among a group of criminals who rob a bank in Paris. During the course of the film, a great deal of tension is created by demonstrating just how corrupt and cruel the band of criminals that Zed has signed on with really are. As the robbery progresses and Zed witnesses just how violent they are, he starts to differentiate himself from them and this becomes apparent to the audience. He isn't truly an anti-hero, as he is engaged in a crime that ends up taking several lives and that he did not become involved in for any good end. But he does redeem himself throughout the course of the film.

Reformed criminal characters work very well as detectives and, in some cases, even as police officers who have enough of a shady background to give themselves something of an edge over the criminals that they encounter.

This type of hero is oftentimes utilized in action films and in thriller films that cross over into the action genre. The primary difference between the reformed criminal in an action film is usually that, in those cases, their actions will be wholly good and the film will endeavor to provide more action sequences than tension and fear. In a thriller film, it's more likely to see a reformed criminal being uncomfortably confronted with the nature of what they have done and to have much of the tension revolve around them having to get out of a bad situation that they may have brought on themselves.

Man, Woman or Both on the Run

Going on the run is a staple of good thriller films. In fact, *Psycho* engages in one of the most sadistic plot twists imaginable, when it transitions from a film about a woman on the run who decides to make right into an incredibly dark and disturbing tale of insanity.

In *North by Northwest*, the plot centers on Roger Thornhill having to make a run for his life over a case of mistaken identity.

As was stated when introducing the elements that make thriller films work, keeping a sense of tension is one of the most important parts of making these films enjoyable. Having a character go on the run is an easy and very effective way to do this. It not only allows the writers and director to create motion and tension on the screen, it also gives them a reason to bring different settings into play, to engage in exciting vehicle chases and more.

The protagonist in a thriller may be on the run for good reasons or bad reasons, but if they do happen to be on the lam it is oftentimes one of the most important elements in the plot.

Just Plain Naïve

Sometimes, the protagonist in a thriller film has no idea what they've gotten themselves into. In *Misery*, for example, Paul Sheldon has absolutely no idea at first that the woman who is tending to him and is seemingly very enamored of his novels, is actually a raging psychopath who embodies the worst traits of an obsessive personality.

In the 2011 science-fiction thriller *Limitless*, there is a fine example of a character who starts out as naïve turning the tables on someone who is exploiting them. Eddie Morra rather naïvely takes an experimental drug that gives him tremendous mental capacity but which, of course, comes with some horrible side effects. While the audience is set up to believe that a corrupt businessman will ultimately end up getting his comeuppance via Morra, that businessman ends up being the one who is naïve about just how masterful Morra has become at controlling his world and the people in it.

In *Jacob's Ladder* the protagonist is completely uncomprehending of what is happening to him. This, in fact, is really what drives the plot forward. His naïveté increases the level of tension in the movie, as the audience is just as mystified as he is as to why his life is taking such bizarre twists. Add into this an apparent government conspiracy, random hallucinations, fevers and other tension building elements and the audience and the protagonist are all taken for a terrifying ride.

Good vs. Evil vs. Reality

In thriller films, it's perfectly acceptable for the antagonist to have genuinely admirable qualities and for the protagonist to be a bit on the shady side. This is what makes these films work. Everybody in these films is drawn from the start as a real human being. Rather than watching cardboard cutout characters get chased through the woods by an ax-wielding madman or watching characters go through rather conventional emotional trials and tribulations, a thriller gives the audience an opportunity to see people brought to the edge. The antagonist may even be among those characters brought to the brink.

In a thriller movie, the limits on a protagonist are only as binding as the limits on the writer's creativity. A protagonist in a thriller film can be an everyman-type character or can be an extraordinary character. A thriller can center on a protagonist who is the embodiment of virtue and who is wholly undeserving of what they go through, such as in the film *Gaslight*, or they can be quite a bit more complex, such as Ms. Crane in *Psycho*.

A good thriller thrives on not presenting the audience with what they expect. This is why, among other reasons, thriller films that have heroes who are far from pure good are so much more interesting than many action films, sci-fi films, horror films and so forth that simply put the hero on one side of the line and the antagonist on the other. In fact, in the world of thriller films, the word "hero" is often inappropriate. Protagonist is usually a more useful term for this genre.

Bonus Chapter:

Sympathy for the Devil

"Please allow me to introduce myself, I'm a man of wealth and taste."

-"Sympathy for the Devil." The Rolling Stones

Sometimes, a thriller movie can make what would seem impossible possible. It can allow people to feel sympathetic toward individuals who, in the context of the story, may be responsible for horrific crimes. This is one of the most intriguing elements of the genre itself. Because it can elicit a feeling of emotion for people who would, in less complex genres, simply be monsters, a thriller film introduces an entirely other type of discomfort.

It's easy enough to think of oneself as a hero when, in one's imaginary world, every vision of a villain is one of somebody in a black hat, wearing a cape and twirling their mustache. Thriller movies, like real life, are much more complex than that. Perhaps the audience hates the villain while they are in the middle of whatever type of crime they are committing, but that same audience may come to sympathize with the villain somewhat when they see how tormented they actually are or, in some cases, when it is revealed that the villain is arguably not even responsible for their own crimes.

None of this complexity should take away from the fact that, sometimes, the villain is simply much cooler than the protagonist.

Sympathy

Imagine for a moment that somebody gave you a thumbnail sketch of the plot of the film *Fatal Attraction*. A man has a torrid affair with a woman who then becomes very attached, perhaps a bit obsessed with him. Because this man is married, he has to cover his own tracks, and to do so, he becomes increasingly rude to the woman, trying to ignore her outright and to pretend she doesn't even exist.

If you have seen the film, you know what happens next. The woman engages in a series of actions that not only cross the line into insanity, they leave it far in the rearview mirror. But, just for a moment, imagine that you had only heard the first part. A man cheats on his wife, the woman he cheats with gets angry because the man now wants to pretend she doesn't exist and she gets obsessive over it. Now, imagine that the woman is your sister, your mother, your daughter or just a female friend.

This is the type of reversal that thriller movies specialize in. While they may take off to a very dark place, they oftentimes start out in a place that is simply shady and it's not always clear that the protagonist isn't the one who is morally or ethically lacking in some regard. In fact, in thriller movies, the protagonists sometimes bring the villain on themselves.

In some cases, a good thriller film can take this even further, giving the audience occasion to sympathize with somebody who is exceptionally dark, even for a thriller movie character. Take, for example, Beckert in *M*. He murders children. There is absolutely no way that any sane human being could have sympathy for such an individual. Or is there?

In that film, which is detailed in a later chapter, there is a scene where the audience, for a moment, could possibly sympathize with Beckert. At the heart of it, he is tormented by what he does. He cannot stop thinking about what he does. He is mortified, disgusted and well aware of the travesty of what he does. He doesn't want to think about it, either. He hates himself, too.

In a lesser film of a lesser genre, the solution to characters like Beckert would be simple. The hero pulls out a gun and, in a moment of glorious, justified violence, the hero would probably put a bullet in the villain's head. They might even put a few bullets somewhere else first, just to make it hurt more. In a thriller, however, the point is to increase tension and discomfort. Having to look at someone as repulsive as a child murderer and realize that they are, despite the ultimate horror of their nature, a human being, is the type of discomfort a thriller film delivers more than anything else. A thriller film such as *M* doesn't ask the audience to condone, but it does force them to understand.

There But for the Grace...

There's a game sociology students are sometimes encouraged to play as a type of thought experiment. Essentially, the idea is to imagine that, if you were born in a different culture, how different of a person would you be? You would obviously have different beliefs and different values, but would you have radically different morals? Would you put those morals into action in a radically different ethical framework?

For most people willing to, at least for a moment, let go of the worship of the individual that is characteristic of Western society, the answer is yes. If someone were born in a different time, different nation or into a different culture, they would likely be a remarkably different person than they are at the moment. That reality is something that can make an audience extremely uncomfortable in a thriller movie and it is most certainly not lost on the writers of these films.

In the film *Cape Fear*, the protagonist and the antagonist both, to some degree, embody this. Max Cady did, in fact, commit a horrific crime, but there was evidence that could've gotten him a lesser sentence. The protagonist, Sam Bowden, made a decision to betray his client and expose him to the harshest possible sentence, based on the severity of the crime.

Either one of these characters could be any member of the audience. Everybody makes mistakes. Certainly, not everyone is a murderer, but Max Cady could have possibly been reformed, could have served out a sentence commensurate with the evidence against him and, at the time of his arrest, he was illiterate, betraying the fact that his options in life were probably rather limited to begin with. He committed a horrific crime but, as real life demonstrates, some people who do commit horrific crimes go on to become people who are not, by any stretch of the imagination, evil. They can be reformed, in some cases.

Sam Bowden, on the other hand, could also be any member of the audience. Confronted with the evidence that he saw and the crime that Cady had committed, it's completely understandable why he may have wanted to see Cady pay, and pay severely, for his violence.

Given that the audience could see themselves in either of these characters, consider what that means for the plot. If someone had gotten you convicted and gotten you a sentence much harsher than you would've otherwise received because they withheld evidence, would revenge be so far from your mind? If you had been raised in the type of environment that Cady likely was, would you know any other way to make things right?

Likewise, if you were Sam Bowden, could you have, with a good conscience, let evidence get into a trial that would've set a murderer free? Even if it was your obligation to offer the best possible defense, could you do so knowing that the defendant was actually guilty?

Thrillers are about making the audience uncomfortable. Nothing achieves this quite as effectively as a moment of moral ambiguity that sets up the characters as real people. While Max Cady does become an obvious example of a very deadly, very motivated and ruthless man, one always must keep in the back of their mind whether that wickedness was forged in a crucible that he could've been spared ever experiencing. If that had been the case, would he have turned out as a good man after all? A flawed person with a distressing background, but there are many such people in the world.

We're Not So Different...

This popular trope even has its own page on the TV Tropes website. In thriller films, it is sometimes used in its classic form, where the villain confronts the hero and points out that, overall, they have more in common than they have separating them. In other films, however, this is used more subtly. Quite often, the way a thriller film will utilize this trope is by confusing the audience as to the real identity of the villain by setting up the protagonist as someone who could actually be the villain.

To Catch a Thief is a good example of this. In the film, John Robie is fleeing from his past as a master cat burglar, but ends up being drawn into a very tense scenario and helping the authorities to actually catch the thief he is accused of being. Throughout the film, Hitchcock does a masterful job of helping the audience to realize that, even though the protagonist is likely not the thief, he was at one time and, overall, there isn't much separating him from the actual thief.

This aspect of villainy has a huge place in spy films and, in fact, some of the finest examples appear in spy films. After all, many of the people who James Bond spends his time going after are ruthless killers who work for shadowy organizations. Bond could easily look in the mirror and find a ruthless killer who works for a shadowy organization, so the idea that he isn't that much different than most of the villains that he pursues is absolutely spot-on.

This is also a major part of the film *Taken*. Liam Neeson's character is clearly every bit as murderous and violent as the human trafficker gang. In fact, given that his background is as a CIA agent, there is a better-than-average chance that he has participated in kidnapping people and spiriting them away to dark corners of the world to have who knows what done to them for whatever reason. There really isn't that much of a difference between what he did for a living and what the villains do, excepting the fact that the villains are doing it to somebody who was entirely innocent. Then again, given what is known about intelligence agency blunders, it's likely that somebody like Bryan Mills has done his fair share of abducting innocent people and subjecting them to tortures, as well.

Falling Down, a 1993 film, centers on a character named William Foster who, after enduring too much stress, finally snaps. When he snaps, he snaps spectacularly and all manner of mayhem ensues. Is he so different than the audience? Hasn't everyone been stuck in traffic at one point or another and fantasized about just leaving their car and being done with it for good? Hasn't everyone gotten rude service at a restaurant at one time or another and literally wanted to physically assault the person responsible for that rude service? William Foster really isn't much different than any other audience member. He's stuck in a monotonous job, has a monotonous life and is frustrated by things that are relatively beyond his control. Eventually, he snaps. In this case, the trope actually works on the audience.

Interestingly, in the movie, there is something of a safety valve for the audience. Confronted by a racist gun shop owner who actually tries to give Foster a version of the "We are not so different..." speech, Foster balks. Foster may be a man who has been pushed over the edge and he may, in fact, be crossing the law as if it were his profession, but he is not motivated by hate. He is much different than the gun shop owner; he knows it, even though he also knows he is going too far. This allows the audience to deal with some of the discomfort the character may have been raising in them and to still sympathize with the protagonist, and it's one of the best moments that anyone is likely to find in a thriller film as far as differentiating the truly hateful from the merely tormented.

In a thriller film, the audience identifies with every element of the story and that is where its power comes from. Oftentimes, part of the power of a thriller comes from the fact that the audience can, to some extent, identify with the antagonist. The antagonist may be someone they can sympathize with because they have been through similar circumstances, the antagonist may be somebody who has just been pushed too far or the antagonist may simply be someone who is as cool as the audience, to some degree, wishes they were.

There's no shame in this. In fact, as the next chapters will reveal, part of what makes a great thriller is allowing the audience to go to some very uncomfortable places in a safe way.

http://tvtropes.org/pmwiki/pmwiki.php/NotSoDifferent/Film

M: Some of the Roots of the Thriller (1931)

Director: Fritz Lang

Starring: Peter Lorre

      Otto Wernicke

      Gustaf Grundgens

M was released in 1931 and directed by Fritz Lang. This film might be old, but the tension and anxiety it raises in the viewer have not diminished a bit. This film is definitely worth watching for any fan of the thriller genre and, in particular, fans of early cinema are likely to be glad they took the hour and 45 minutes this film lasts out of their lives to experience one of the best early thriller films.

Plot and Story

M tells the story of a child murderer in 1930s Berlin. At the beginning of the film, he's already a wanted man, but no one knows his identity. The first 10 minutes of this film are absolutely masterful in how they bring up the level of tension.

A child, Elsie, is walking down a Berlin street playing with her ball. The shot changes to a wanted poster—in German, but there are subtitled versions of this film—that warns of a child murderer. A shadow falls over the poster; the profile of a man, and it's obvious what the message of this shot happens to be.

In thriller films, what the audience doesn't see is oftentimes more terrifying than what they do see. The killer buys Elsie a balloon. Her mom calls out for her, but she's not there. Elsie doesn't make it to dinner; her ball rolls through the frame. She is dead and, without showing a drop of blood or recording a single scream, Lang has made the scenario unfold in a way more disturbing than it probably would have been had he actually shown the murder.

The next scenes show the city reacting; newspapers alerting the populace to the crime are being distributed. Who is the murderer?

The murderer, in classic serial killer fashion, writes letters to let the authorities know he isn't finished and that the murders will continue. At the point when the movie opens up, he has killed 8 children already and he clearly intends to kill more.

This setup begins some of the classic elements that make this film so definitive as an early thriller.

The Shark in the Water

Figure 2: The killer casts his shadow.

When discussing the thriller genre, one of the most effective storytelling devices to keep in mind is putting the shark in the water, but not letting the audience see it as soon as they'd like. There is a threat and the players—as well as the audience—know as much, but not much more.

In the film *M*, Lang sets us up magnificently from the opening moments. The audience doesn't see the killer to begin with, merely his profile cast on the wanted poster seeking information about him. The little girl sees the killer, but she obviously isn't in a position to do anything with that knowledge and, in fact, is only the latest of his victims, as the poster against which she bounces her ball in the opening scenes reveals.

Lang ratchets up the tension by making certain that there is as little chance as possible that any character would be able to identify the child murderer walking with poor Elsie Beckmann. The killer baits the child by offering to purchase her a balloon, but he buys that balloon from a blind street vendor, eliminating the chances of the vendor being able to render a description to the police.

In a thriller film, the killer is sometimes shown to have a trademark or an outright giveaway that is demonstrated early on. While nobody may know who M really is at the beginning of the film, he does whistle "In the Hall of the Mountain King", a piece by Edvard Grieg, while he purchases the balloon. Of course, the particular piece he is whistling features a group of trolls calling out to kill a man who has brought the daughter of the Mountain King under his spell. This song will play a part in events during the climax of the film.

Paranoia

Despite the fact that it was made over 80 years ago, *M* is still engaging in the way the plot unfolds. One of the first scenes to which the audience is treated is a group of men sitting around a table reading a newspaper together. Gradually, as they read about the horrible murders in the news, paranoia takes over.

It isn't long before one of the men is casting suspicions on another and an argument erupts. This is a hallmark of a good thriller film. In order to keep tension high among the audience members, the director and the writers have to ensure that the players are exhibiting signs of tension and one of the best ways to do that is to show paranoia.

Nobody knows who the killer is at this point in the movie. He has already claimed several children, there is a reward out for him and, of course, he represents the most reprehensible sort of murderer imaginable. He is the murderer who destroys the truly innocent, who, as the newspaper says, utilizes candy or toys as weapons against his victims—metaphorically, he uses such items to *bait* his victims, not to assault them—and who defies something so foundational to society—the protection of children—that his mere presence cannot help but introduce severe paranoia.

The newspaper article points out that it is the duty of parents—women, specifically, given the sexism of the time—to watch over their children. The child murderer is not only a threat to individual children, he is a threat to the traditional role of a parent and to society as a whole. Cohesion breaks down. Friends reading a newspaper together suddenly start throwing accusations of murder at one another. Children aren't safe.

The killer's shadow, in the beginning of the film, looms across the wanted poster seeking information about him, symbolically casting darkness over the attempts of the authorities to bring his identity to light. It's not long before there are examples of the weak and unattractive being accused by vigilant, bullying men, desperately wanting to protect society. In the presence of this murderer, the inability of parents to protect their children against a menacing threat is revealed and, in some scenes, the attempts of society at large to protect itself turn into examples of buffoonery that are embarrassing at best and terrifying at worst. When the structure is threatened, it's not long before the mob takes charge.

The Fin above the Water

The tension in *M* is maintained by steadily revealing small details about the killer. This is oftentimes accomplished in this film by showing the investigation underway, keeping the story moving forward and the killer front and center.

While *M* has the hallmarks of any modern, gritty crime thriller, some of what takes place on-screen is obviously outdated. For example, the police are shown using techniques including handwriting analysis to try to identify the killer. Essentially, between lifting fingerprints off the letters that he sends to the newspaper and analyzing his handwriting, they are engaging in a nearly century-old version of

The Thrillers

what modern detectives would call profiling. What did they find? More threats to traditional morality and order.

While handwriting analysis has long been debunked as a way of psychologically profiling people—it's about as effective as reading tea leaves—at the time there was some belief in it and, moreover, it provides a convenient plot element that allows the writer to give the viewer an idea of the killer's personality.

The killer is cast as someone with a strong sexual deviancy. Obviously, this threatens the traditional order immediately and makes the implication that there is some sort of pedophilia involved in the murderer's motivations. The handwriting, according to the detectives, also reveals that the killer has "an actor's personality." He's someone who isn't what he appears to be. He's a hidden threat. In terms of affronting traditional notions of morality, he doesn't fight fair or with honor. He murders the innocent and does so in the most cowardly fashion imaginable, not even having the honor to reveal himself and, in doing so, possibly save the lives of children he may have otherwise murdered. He is an ultimate corruption of the parental instinct.

The killer is also cast as being indolent or even lazy. Of course, because the notion of a work ethic is so important to the traditions of people all over the world, this is another affront to the traditional order.

To put it in less ornate terms, the killer is a lazy, cowardly liar who preys on children, who also probably has some sort of sexual interaction with them and, of course, who is likely insane. Moreover, the killer is insane in a way that makes it extremely difficult for any rational person to have any degree of sympathy for him as one would, perhaps, for someone who is simply schizophrenic and tormented, but not violent or dangerous in any way.

The detectives work earnestly to track down the killer, and there is an interesting setup that is characteristic of many thriller films that would follow. The detectives are demonstrated—through conversation with the Minister—to be using the most scientific methods possible to track down the killer. They methodically search every area related to the crime, even going so far as to recover grains of sugar that came from candy the killer bought for a child. They expand the area in which they search in precise, concentric circles, interviewing every person who could've seen anything, literally leaving no stone unturned. Yet, it is all for naught.

People's emotions run high. Two men argue over whether the Beckmann girl was wearing a red hat or a green hat, a pointless argument that only reveals that neither of them really took the time to pay attention to the people around them. No matter how much the police apply the traditional methods of rational investigation, scientific analysis and a diligent, relentless and—by traditional standards—honorable work ethic, they are frustrated by the wild emotions, faulty memories and human infirmities that are brought to the surface by this murderous and, in fact, existential threat to the existing order.

The Investigation: Instant Tension

One of the truly remarkable things about the film *M* is how it utilizes what amount to very primitive techniques by modern standards to tell an incredibly effective story. This is exemplified in the revealing of the police investigation.

It's also important to keep in mind that filmmaking in the 1930s was very primitive compared to what filmmakers have available to them now, or had even two decades later when Hitchcock was crafting his masterpieces. A series of shots is interspersed throughout the beginning of the film showing investigators searching for clues, pounding the pavement and even employing dogs to try to track down a scent. They remain, of course, frustrated, but this is an excellent (and rather clever, considering the technology) way to demonstrate the sheer terror that is taking over Berlin in the face of these child murders.

This procedural element allows the audience to get an idea of how much time and effort is being expended into the investigation. Not only does the investigation ratchet up the tension in terms of demonstrating just how much the murderer has impacted the community, it shows how community bonds have broken down in the face of his crimes.

For example, the narrator reveals that the police have regularly been searching the establishments where vagrants spend their nights, called flophouses at the time. Even in 1930s Germany, there was concern that this was breaking down the relationship between the police and the citizens on the whole. While the police—particularly in Europe during that era—had powers that would likely be considered tools of oppression today, there was still a traditional order between the police and the citizenry that allowed both to function. The murderer is a threat to that. The investigation demonstrates the tension but also, within the story itself, creates tension where none would normally exist or, if it did, where the tension would be relegated to a tension between police and outlaws. That last element becomes vitally important to how the story unfolds.

More than Just Police Technology

CS Film Analysis points out that sound was relatively new at the time that *M* was filmed. It's used to great effect in the film, despite its newness at the time. There isn't a soundtrack on the film, which will stand out to modern audiences who are accustomed to the music telling them how they should feel about what's going on in a film.

In the scenes that open up the film, where Elsie's mother is calling for her, the silence of her apartment and the stairway are downright oppressive. In a modern film, there may very well have been a soundtrack added that would've let the audience know they were supposed to feel tension and, even more so, that soundtrack may have increased and decreased in tension and changed in other suggestive ways as the scenes cut back and forth. While this can be a very effective storytelling technique, it does take away from what the audience is allowed to do in terms of filling in the blanks in their own minds, which can actually make a scene tenser.

In that first scene, the feeling is really one of ambivalence and dread more than it is outright tension. The audience knows that Elsie has decided to go with a man who will ultimately kill her. It's easy to step into the shoes of the mother for a moment, however, and realize how she must be feeling. She's probably not filled with dread, but she is certainly anxious about her missing child. The child hasn't been gone long enough when the scenes take place to make it obvious that something is wrong, but she's clearly not coming home as expected, and she's missing supper. There's enough here for the mother to have a very justified feeling of anxiety, but the absence of a soundtrack almost adds to it, as the audience, along with the mother, is forced to endure the horribly oppressive silence of the apartment building to which Elsie never returns.

As the aforementioned analysis points out, as well, various techniques involving narration are heavily utilized in this film. Quite often, characters are portrayed reading material to other characters. This allows for a very clever way of giving the audience exposition and allowing the audience, at the same time, to get a perfect perspective on what the characters actually know about what's going on. The audience does know more than the characters. Because of this device of having one character read to another—on the street, in the room while the men are smoking pipes and on the telephone between the police and other authorities, among other instances—the audience is also able to participate in the process the characters go through as they gradually begin to understand who the killer is, what motivates him and how they may be able to track him down before he kills again.

Some of the aspects of this film might seem a bit slow-moving to modern viewers because of the technology used and some of the shooting techniques. There isn't music to spice up the affair, of course, and the dialog moves at a pace more common in the early days of film. That is to say, there's a lot of talking in *M* and it sometimes reiterates the same things repeatedly. Nevertheless, the film is masterful and the way that the film is shot differs from modern techniques enough to make it very interesting to watch.

Enjoying the Film

If you're in the mood for something truly different, *M* is likely to deliver. The movie succeeds in creating the tension that a thriller needs, the subject matter is really quite morbid—especially considering the era—and there's a lot left to the imagination here. Don't expect a nice, clean ending with this one. The ambiguity carries over into how the film eventually ends and the fate of the murderer, Hans Beckert. Peter Lorre's performance is excellent. He's genuinely creepy.

The Absence of Effects and Thrillers

Thrillers are really story-driven films. This is on display in this film, given that there really isn't anything that modern audiences would describe as special effects. One way to contrast a pure thriller from a more effective driven genre, such as a sci-fi thriller or pure sci-fi, is observable in *M*. The movie manages to be an effective thriller, despite the limitations that filmmakers had to deal with at the time. Compared to some of the earliest sci-fi and sci-fi thrillers, it's easy to see how the lacking effects technology of the time held some of those films back from being as engaging as they could have otherwise been. It's difficult to feel tension when you know the biggest threat in a film is a monster that's obviously made out of rubber, for instance. In *M*, the tension is generated by pure storytelling and that makes it just as engaging to watch now as it was when it was released, eight decades ago. Few films are likely to hold up for so long.

Gaslight: Driven Insane (1944)

Director: Gregory Anton

Starring: George Cukor

Gregory Anton

Ingrid Bergman

Joseph Cotten

Ingrid Bergman won an Oscar for her role as the protagonist, Paula Alquist, in *Gaslight*. Her performance is a significant part of why this film works. Adapted from several stage plays, the story unfolds in Victorian London, in the era where the titular gaslights were the norm in households and on London streets. Alquist is an opera singer who falls in love with one of the best movie cads you'll find anywhere. What ensues, however, is far from melodrama. It's visceral, sympathy-inducing and very tense and, at times, very hard to watch, given what happens to poor Paula during the film.

The Plot and Setup

Paula's mother, also an opera singer, was murdered when she was a child, and this is the opening of the film. The murderer was a robber who was after jewels that he knew to be part of Alice Aliquist's possessions. He didn't manage to get them, but he does manage to get away from the authorities.

Paula is haunted by this memory, but she spends her time honing her craft as an opera singer, already setting up a significant parallel between mother and daughter in the story. She meets Gregory Anton, a smooth, cultured man who she falls for and ends up marrying. She relocates back to London from Italy so that they can live together. The home is classic Gothic in its trappings. It is dark, cavernous and, given the gas lighting, very dim and ruled by shadows.

The game that Anton intends to play begins immediately and focuses on a note that Paula finds. The note was written just before the murder of her mother and Gregory gets very angry when she sees it, implying that he has something to hide.

Paula is subjected to a vicious metal game. Anton begins to manipulate her by taking items from her and from around the house and then claiming that she actually did it. She begins to doubt her own memory and, of course, this is precisely what Anton wants from her.

Anton's goal is to drive Paula completely mad. Once she is certified as such, he will become the owner of the home. Anton is actually the same would-be jewel thief who murdered Paula's mother. He knows that the jewels he is after are still in Alice's possessions, which Paula has stored in the attic of her London townhouse. If he can get Paula committed, Anton can continue his quest for the jewels, getting both Paula's possessions and the priceless items he has been wanting to get his hands on for over a decade.

Anton has a very slick exterior and a slimy interior, perfect for a manipulative villain. He starts getting Paula to question not only her memory, but whether she's having delusions. The gas lighting used at the time only had so much pressure in the lines to work with. Turn on the lights in one room and the lighting in the other rooms would dim. Paula keeps seeing this happen, indicating that there is someone else in the house, but Anton keeps telling her that she imagined it. This starts to make Paula question her sanity even more, giving her a deep fear that she is losing her mind.

Paula also begins to hear footsteps on the ceiling, which Anton explains is a symptom of her suffering from some sort of mental illness.

Paula begins to break down. To make things worse, Anton starts to isolate her, reminiscent of the resting cure references in the short story *The Yellow Wallpaper*. Without anyone else to talk to and with Anton abusing her mentally at every turn, Paula begins to slip into self-doubt, depression and anxiety. She is not insane, but she's starting to think that she most certainly is.

Paula convinces Anton to go to a recital so that she can get some socialization in. At the recital, Anton sets her up by putting his watch in her purse without her knowing and then, during the recital, showing her the watch chain in his vest, from which the watch has been removed. Paula digs through her purse and finds it, breaking down in front of the entire crowd and causing a scene. This is one of the scenes in this film that truly makes the audience detest Anton. In addition to trying to crush his wife's sanity, he isolates her, intends to steal from her and adds public humiliation to the list of ills he does. He is thoroughly and truly evil. He makes it even worse by using her outburst at the recital as a way to justify keeping her even more isolated.

Unbeknownst to Paula, she has someone in her corner who knows that something isn't right with Anton. A detective from Scotland Yard, Cameron, has earlier begun tailing Anton, though Anton isn't sure as to what's going on. While following him through one of the famously foggy London nights, he finds that Anton has disappeared into an alley that offers access to his own home from a back way. He puzzles over it, but it's apparent that he starts to understand what's going on in this scene.

What makes this movie interesting, particularly for a movie of its time period, is that Cameron is not so much the hero at the end of the film as the one who verifies to Paula that she is not going insane, allowing her to bring about big revenge during the final moments of the film. While one of the housekeepers at Paula's home seems not to like her at all, the other, older, housekeeper does and has suspicions about what Anton is up to. She helps the detective to snare him in the end.

There are some incredible moments in this film that make it a great thriller.

The Isolation Treatment

Thrillers are best when they raise tension levels via realistic scenarios. Anton acts like the classic domestic abuser. He does two things that really define a great deal of domestic abuse that is visited upon women:

- He completely isolates his wife, placing himself in control
- He makes his wife question her sanity, silencing her protests by implying that she's incompetent

This has the effect of really, really making the audience hate Anton. Not only is he a thief and a murderer, he's a sadist on top of it. He seems to get real joy out of hurting Paula and, given that this woman grew up after watching her mother be murdered, she's already suffered enough for anyone. She's a good person, as well, and Bergman portrays her in a way that makes the audience want to swoop in and save her, and maybe take Anton out in the process.

Anton is an extreme case, but the abuse he visits upon Paula is such a classic example of this particular type of abuse that it has become acknowledged as a real thing. As *Psychology Today* points out excellently, "gaslighting" is a form of abuse that takes time and that allows your abuser to "define your reality." This is exactly what Anton is doing. Paula is a sweet, kind person with a great deal of talent who has become as much despite the hardships that she has suffered. This is her reality. Her reality, however, as Anton begins to define it for her, is of a woman who is slowly but surely losing her mind, who hallucinates intruders in her home and who steals things without remembering. In Anton's self-serving reality, Paula is an untrustworthy basket case who is probably on the fast track to an asylum and only being isolated and controlled by Anton himself can serve as a means for her to save herself.

If you hate this guy soon into the film, it's only because you're paying attention.

This particular thriller also has strong elements of Gothic horror in it. It involves a beautiful, innocent woman who is held captive in what is, for all intents and purposes, an impregnable castle. It makes heavy use of dim lighting, shadow play, menace and insanity to elicit its thrills, making it a great example of how thrillers can borrow from any genre, even the Gothic, to create a marvelous and memorable tale.

Mental Games

In order to set up the plot, the story does a bit of foreshadowing that demonstrates that Paula, however much she may have made of herself, has not completely gotten beyond her past. She takes a train trip and visits with a woman who talks to her about murder mysteries, something that Paula has obvious reasons to avoid. The woman even brings up the murder itself, causing Paula to be disturbed by the thought, as she probably has been throughout her entire life.

Paula is also reaching out for someone to comfort her, a role that Anton readily, however dishonestly, seems willing to provide in her life. She feels comfortable around him, protected. She doesn't see the danger in him and has no idea that, for 10 years, this man has been looking to get to her. Paula's mother was murdered by what amounts to an intergenerational predator and thief and, to make it worse, he's already set up his ambush.

When Paula does return home to London, parts of the house remind her of death. She has a difficult time with certain rooms and the home holds a menace all its own. She is unnerved in many ways before Anton even begins toying with her, making her a perfect victim for what he has in mind.

Were Paula more in control of her emotions, it would probably be hard to believe that Anton could pull this game off. After all, she knows that there's an attic in the home and the natural thing to do would be to go up there every time she heard footsteps, or to call for the police. She's already fearful, however, and this allows Anton to proceed with his games.

Anton's real name is Sergis Bauer. He had actually written the note to her mother that Paula found, which explains why he became so enraged when she found it. Again, he writes off his explosion as him simply being concerned for Paula's wellbeing, fixing her in his trap even more effectively.

Anton, however, doesn't realize that he has met his match. The Scotland Yard detective has been shadowing them since the game started with Paula's disappearing brooch during a scene at the Tower of London. He had his suspicions right away.

The detective also happens to have been a fan of Paula's mother, giving him a personal interest in the case. He plans to figure out what's going on but, in the way that this story resolves, we get to see Paula vindicate herself and transcend the victim role.

Paula Gets Her Revenge

Watching Paula realize that she's been manipulated is painful. Bergman pulls it off masterfully, coming off as a genuine victim of abuse who didn't even know she was being abused, an all too familiar and tragic reality of life. The detective breaks into Anton's desk and finds the missing brooch, the letter—which Anton has convinced her never existed—and, worst of all, a missing handgun.

In the meantime, Anton has finally found the objects of his quest. While he may have the air of someone who thinks of themselves as a master manipulator and an intellectual heavyweight, he is revealed to be something of a fool. Alice had hidden her priceless jewels in plain sight, sewing them into a costume gown along with costume jewelry. Anton seems to have won at this point, but he's the one who is confused about reality now.

Cameron wants justice and leaves the house, going out to look for Anton. He assures the head housekeeper, who has been sympathetic to Paula all along, that "the master" won't be returning. Of course, the master does return and immediately begins trying to gaslight Paula all over again. This time, he tries to convince her that the detective didn't exist and the head housekeeper seems to play along, ironically gaslighting Anton himself.

The detective shows up, however, and is prepared to arrest Anton. Anton makes a break for it but is tied to a chair after a struggle in the attic with the detective and a bobby. Paula, against the wishes and advice of Cameron, wants to confront her tormentor and the scene that follows is one of the most satisfying instances of a truly bad person getting their comeuppance from their victim.

Anton asks Paula to cut the ropes. She grabs a knife and holds it about as menacingly as anyone has ever held a knife in a film. Then the real fun begins.

Paula turns Anton's game on its head. She tosses the knife and says that it must have been imaginary. She's mad, she says. She berates him, torments him by implying that she will cut him loose but doesn't. In the end, she simply calls in the detectives, who take him away, likely to death row.

Paula doesn't just defeat her abuser in this scene, she utterly destroys and thoroughly mocks him. She not only makes it clear that his plan has been an abysmal failure, but that he, himself, is an abysmal failure. He's a thief who has failed to steal the same jewelry for over a decade, in essence, and who now is humiliated by having the daughter of his victim, and one of his victims in his own right, rub his face in it. It's a great moment in a great film.

Why This Film Works

Gaslight is haunting. The way it's shot is haunting. The house is huge, dark and oppressive and symbolic of the death that Paula has been trying to get away from her entire life. The house itself adds to the tension and the fixtures themselves become symbols to Paula of her own insanity and to the audience of just how awful Anton is.

This film also retains the subtlety that makes thrillers so effective. After a while, and particularly at the end of the film, it becomes difficult to tell who's really fooling who. If the film had been, in the end, revealed to be from Paula's perspective, perhaps the detective *was* just a hallucination. It would be a stretch for the audience to have accepted this, but it's not for Paula. She may be on her way to recovering from Anton's abuse, but it's a long road and she's only taken her first steps at this point. She still doubts her sanity, up until almost the very end.

Anton is a great villain. He is not at all the sympathetic villain, however. He's almost a more sadistic and less effective version of Hannibal Lecter. He's brilliant, accustomed to moving around at the highest levels of society but is also someone who clearly is just a heartless predator at his core.

This film is an excellent example of an early thriller and one of the best to be found in an era outside of Hitchcock. It has all the mood necessary to keep the audience edgy. Bergman also succeeds in making the audience want to rescue her without for a moment coming off as the helpless damsel in distress. The real terror of this movie is that even the strongest of people would be likely to collapse under the weight of the abuse that poor Paula suffered. She manages not only to survive it, but she survives it on top of surviving the brutal murder of her own mother. On the surface, this film may seem to be yet another thriller about a woman being victimized by a truly wicked villain. In reality, it's about a very strong woman who is victimized, but who shows a strength of spirit that is uncommon, to say the least.

One of the truly engaging things about good thrillers is that, even in bygone eras where sexism was rampant and cruel, they are movies that aren't afraid to have a strong female character who saves herself. Just as Eve Kendall in *North by Northwest* and Lisa Fremont from *Rear Window* were capable and clever women, Paula Alquist is someone to be admired and respected. It's not the weakness and self-doubt that this character is forced to endure that defines her; it's the ability to survive in a world full of people who want to exploit her—and even take her life from her—that make her who she is. Her story, quite simply put, is thrilling to watch unfold.

http://www.psychologytoday.com/blog/power-in-relationships/200905/are-you-being-gaslighted

Rear Window: A View to a Killer (1954)

Director: Alfred Hitchcock

Starring: James Stewart

Grace Kelly

Wendell Corey

Thelma Ritter

Raymond Burr

Hitchcock is renowned for his ability to create tension, and *Rear Window* is a fine example of this. It is a remarkable movie in many regards, but the setting is likely what will stand out the most to viewers. The entire film takes place in an apartment in New York during a hot summer. Despite this limited location, Hitchcock manages to present the viewer with a compelling story that likely has more punch than a modern viewer might expect, given that this film dates back to 1954. Don't let the era fool you. This film is as tense as anything you're likely to find today and it patiently builds suspense in a way that makes it seem all the more so, since the plot is simple and uncontrived enough to be wholly believable.

The Plot and Setup

Hitchcock uses his trademark voyeuristic camera work right from the beginning of this film and the way it's done demonstrates his mastery of filmmaking craft. We learn the backstory within the space of a few shots. L.B. Jefferies is a photographer and a famous one at that. He has recently been injured in his line of work, apparently having been involved a race car wreck accident that took the life of one of his cameras, shown in a sad state of affairs in these shots. Jefferies has a broken leg, a full-leg cast and is stuck in a wheelchair while he recovers.

Jefferies is very ornery at the beginning of the film, as is revealed through his characters talks with a nurse, Stella, who is taking care of him during his convalescence. Given that Jefferies is accustomed to frequent globe-hopping adventures, it's no wonder that he's out of sorts. He's taken to watching his neighbors through their windows to amuse himself, making up stories to go along with what he sees and, the longer he watches them, becoming more familiar with the rhythm of their lives and their actual activities during the day and night.

Initially, the only real vibe of the film as far as what the main character is feeling centers on boredom and frustration. Jefferies is, in some regards, a rather unpleasant fellow, given his predilection for spying on his neighbors. He graduates from binoculars to a powerful camera lens during the movie and makes up names for his neighbors. They include Miss Torso, an attractive, athletic woman, and Miss Lonelyheart, a sympathetic character whose life seems to fit nicely with her nickname.

Among his neighbors is also a travelling jewelry salesman, Lars Thorwald, played by Raymond Burr, who becomes the focus of the story. Burr was a bear of a man and he plays the role perfectly. While his occupation and his taking care of his wife, who is a shut-in, may make him seem entirely normal, his sheer size does make him intimidating enough to be an effective, if remote, antagonist.

The other main character in this film is Lisa Fremont, played by Grace Kelly. Lisa is very much a city girl and she's in love with Jefferies. Jefferies has wanderlust and doesn't believe that Lisa, who seems delicate and glamorous in the extreme, could hold up to the challenges that his lifestyle presents and rebuffs her interest in taking their relationship further. She wants to travel with him and be a part of his life. Jefferies is ornery enough that he tells Grace Kelly—not exactly a bad catch—that he's not interested in being her permanent squeeze and, perhaps, husband, which is no small thing, given that she's breathtakingly beautiful and already quite taken with him.

Jefferies has some back and forth with Lisa about whether or not he should really be spying on his neighbors and, up until the plot really gets moving, he's pretty much just being voyeuristic. Then, one night, everything changes.

On an appropriately dark and stormy night, Jefferies hears a scream, followed by the sound of something shattering. The menace starts up immediately. Thorwald, travelling salesman that he is, is equipped with a large, metal sample case. Jefferies watches as he goes to and from the house over and over again in the small hours, carrying his case through a torrential rainstorm.

Obviously, something is not right.

It just gets more sinister from there on out. Soon enough, Thorwald is observed cleaning off a butcher knife and saw and wrapping them in newspaper. Then Jefferies sees him tie up a large trunk with rope, which is picked up by movers.

Lisa starts joining in with the obsession. She notes that Mrs. Thorwald wouldn't have taken a long trip—one of the possible justifications for what is going on—without having taken her jewelry with her. Her insights increase Jefferies's suspicions, adding fuel to the fire.

Eventually, Thorwald does get caught, but the way that this movie builds up to its climax is really quite remarkable. This is widely considered to be one of Hitchcock's best movies and, given that he's renowned for his string of excellent films, that's saying something.

Involvement and Voyeurism

There are many different ways that *Rear Window* can be interpreted. Toward the end of the film, in fact, we're treated to a rather fantastic monologue about the value of being neighborly by a woman whose dog is killed, which becomes a major plot point. There is a very strong element of voyeurism here and, as Roger Ebert noted, this film also plays into how someone can place themselves into the role of helplessness, even though he or she may be able to play an active role in resolving a situation. There is also a rather interesting way to interpret parts of this movie and, to some extent, the movie as a whole.

Watching out of his rear window, Jefferies sees what looks like a collection of movie screens plastered across the walls of neighboring apartments. These screens—his neighbor's windows, of course—even have close to the right proportions, in some cases. Jefferies watches as the drama of everyday life unfolds before him. Each window is a different story. Miss Torso is a tease of sorts, doing exercises and looking about as inviting as anyone could. She seems to be happy enough, but she's also bored and waiting on someone to come home.

Miss Lonelyheart is another story entirely. Her tale is bleak and every bit as lonely as her nickname implies. Her story is a drama, a story of a woman who is declining into her own isolation and forever looking for a way to get out of it. As her tale unfolds, we see one of the most obvious examples of when Jefferies really should do something but delays longer than any reasonable person would.

A piano player is shown working out songs and playing for parties. His story is the youthful, dynamic story of an artist in the city, trying to make a name for himself. His story and Miss Lonelyheart's will intertwine during the course of the film. Hitchcock, as much as he liked to keep an audience on edge, was also careful to add genuinely sweet moments to his films. Rather than watering them down, these moments tend to make the films more realistic. After all, it is far more likely that you'll see random acts of kindness on any given city street than you will random acts of murder.

The real action, however, is in Thorwald's apartment. In a way, the audience is watching Jefferies watch what amounts to a film within a film. The central character in the story may be Jefferies, but it's what he's seeing that drives the film forward.

When taken this way, it's easy to see the brilliance in this film. Hitchcock, as was mentioned, very much liked to employ voyeuristic camera techniques that involved the viewer in the story. In this film, it's Jefferies' camera and binoculars that act as the camera and the effect is magnificent. We watch Jefferies watch someone else, but we see it through his eyes, so we're involved.

Moreover, we're also the inactive voyeurs, though we're one level above Jefferies. From this omniscient perspective, we don't have the restrictions on our knowledge of what's going on that Jefferies does, which is rather driven home in the shots through the binoculars and camera, where the edges of the screen are blacked out to give the appearance of the lens. In other regards, however, we're just as restricted as Jefferies. We never move out of his apartment and share his courtyard view. For all intents and purposes, the audience may as well be looking over Jefferies' shoulder as he looks over the courtyard. The effect is that pronounced and that well-executed.

The Complexity of Jefferies

Jefferies is not a bad guy, but he's really irritable. He snaps at his fiancée, tends to be a bit too permissive with himself as far as spying on his neighbors goes and underestimates the people around him almost as a habit. He complains constantly and sometimes outright ignores Lisa in favor of watching whatever's going on outside his window. Lisa gets rebuffed a lot in this film and there is good reason to wonder why she even bothers staying on with Jefferies. Lisa is obviously successful, she's a dress designer and she's very active socially. Jefferies lives in a dingy Greenwich Village apartment and uses every excuse in the book not to let Lisa much further into his life, even though most of those reasons are assumptions regarding her strength as a person.

These things all make Jefferies likeable.

Jefferies is someone who is relatable. He's not a hero, though he is certainly adventurous. He's not built like, nor does he behave like, a fighter—nor is he really capable of doing much, given his broken leg and cast—but he is courageous when the situation calls for it. There are genuine questions this character raises as to how much of modern interaction with our neighbors is purely voyeuristic amusement and how much is genuine relationship-forging, but those are questions that anyone's life likely brings to light.

Jefferies lives an interesting life, is good at what he does and is a veteran, so he isn't afraid of a fight, obviously. He's endured far worse hardships than a broken leg, but it's likely that he complained an awful lot when going through those hardships as well. Jefferies has enough flaws to make him someone the audience can care about and that helps propel the movie forward.

Jefferies does regard himself as being rather clever, it seems. Part of the tension in this film is the fact that, ultimately, the audience knows he is going to get busted at his voyeur game and it's only a matter of time before he, essentially, stirs up a hornet's nest simply by standing there and watching it too long.

Lisa Is Awesome

Lisa (Grace Kelly) certainly could have gotten by in her life on her looks alone. Particularly at the time when this movie is set—the 1950s—anyone looking for a housewife would have been more than happy to have married Lisa. She's stunning, cultured and intelligent, but there's more to her than that.

Kelly's character is a successful dressmaker. She has her own credentials and has proven herself to be capable of excellence. She could have just gone the route of finding someone rich to pamper her, but she's got substance to her beneath her style.

Lisa also proves herself to be incredibly brave during the climax of the film. She delivers a letter to Thorwald's door after its obvious to anyone that he did, in fact, murder his wife. She even climbs from a fire escape landing to Thorwald's windowsill—petticoats and all—risking killing herself to get into the apartment and gather evidence. When she realizes that Thorwald's wife's wedding ring was left behind, and that no woman of the time would have left without it on, she becomes determined to seize it as evidence. In the middle of being arrested for breaking and entering and after being physically assaulted by Thorwald in his apartment, she still has the presence of mind not only to slip the wedding band on her own finger, securing the evidence, but to waggle it in Jefferies's field of view so he knows that she got it.

There's a lot to like about Lisa's character. She has the patience to put up with Jefferies, which is a feat in and of itself, and she has the presence of mind to perform under pressure. She's willing to risk life and limb to bring a murderer to justice, and even willing to risk a confrontation with a very large, imposing man in the process.

Lisa is probably the person who Jefferies underestimates the most. In the end of the film, we see her reclining in a pair of jeans and reading a travel magazine, apparently showing that Jefferies and Lisa will be taking some journeys together. Ironically enough, while Jefferies could piece together an entire murder plot by watching the participants through binoculars, he didn't see what he had right in front of him. Unlike poor Mrs. Thorwald, Jefferies does manage to see what he has before he loses everything.

Interestingly, as Dramatica.com points out, the first time we see Lisa in the film is in a slide viewer and she's shown in the negative. This is how Jefferies sees her, even though, as the analysis points out, he does like some of the things that would go along with marriage. He acts curmudgeonly toward Lisa, but she keeps showing up and she provides someone to listen to what, at first, seem to be wild theories he's concocted. She calms him down and softens his edges when he gets too worked up. When dealing with Doyle, Jefferies' war buddy who became a police detective, Lisa backs Jefferies up and provides a very rational, well-considered argument as to why Jefferies may be right. Of course, given that this is the 1950s, Doyle dismisses her by asking her to get everyone a drink.

Lisa puts up with a lot and, at the end of the film, she's still the one with the guts to stop being a voyeur, trust her and Jefferies' instincts and to successfully confront, and actually out, a killer. Jefferies may have run out on a racetrack and gotten his leg broken in the line of work, but Lisa proves to be no less courageous and, despite all the evidence of as much that's staring him right in the face, Jefferies has a hard time seeing it.

Doyle

Doyle is a police detective who Jefferies knows from their wartime military service. The men clearly have a deep bond, but Doyle primarily serves as a foil, exposing the holes in Jefferies's theories. In an odd way, he is to Jefferies as Jefferies is to Lisa. Jefferies presents him with evidence, all of which points toward a particular conclusion, but Doyle rebuffs it as, after all, Jefferies is no law enforcement officer. He's just a guy at a window with a broken leg, a lot of high-power lenses and too much time on his hands.

As the case against Thorwald becomes more convincing, Doyle's skepticism moves from healthy questioning of the facts to bullheadedness to outright comic relief. Lisa is right; Mrs. Thorwald would not have gone on a trip without her wedding ring. She wouldn't have thrown her jewelry haphazardly in a bag, as women sometimes have a tremendous amount of wealth, and certainly a personal investment, in their jewelry. Why would anyone wrap up a saw and a butcher knife in newspaper? According to Doyle, it's just a knife and even Jefferies has probably owned "hundreds" of knives throughout his lifetime.

Doyle is only convinced when literally presented with the head of Mrs. Thorwald, which Mr. Thorwald had placed in a hatbox. He's intransigent, thick-headed in some ways but, like Jefferies, he is brave and very good at his job. He's a tough guy in an era where being a tough guy generally meant—at least according to what one sees in the films of the time—that you needed to be certain that you were never wrong, even if it took arguing with people who directly contradicted you and who were obviously right.

Doyle can also be seen as something of a symbolic character. He has the authority, the backup and the knowledge that allows him to decide to take action when necessary. Jefferies is rather incapable of doing so, given his leg, and his taking action is further delayed by

Doyle's not taking him seriously. Just as Jefferies is too slow to react to some situations in the movie, Doyle provides another source of frustration for the audience and another example of the audience knowing exactly what's going on and being flustered by a character who refuses to act on solid information. Speaking of…

Miss Lonelyheart

Miss Lonelyheart is obviously pining for someone to take an interest in her and, perhaps, for something to take an interest in for herself. Her biggest role in the story comes near the climax.

Miss Lonelyheart, in action simultaneous with what's going on in Thorwald's apartment above hers, has finally brought a man home. He seems interested but, as they sit down together on the couch, he becomes very aggressive. As he starts showing every intention of crossing the line into rape, and certainly having crossed the line in terms of what most modern people would consider to be sexual assault, Mrs. Lonelyheart manages to drive him out.

We see her, in scenes that follow, pull out far too many sleeping pills, which Jefferies' nurse recognizes through the binoculars. We see her pull out a Bible, as well, and sit down on the couch, resigned.

She's later shown writing a note. Only someone with the most lacking knowledge of human behavior wouldn't know what she was up to. She's broken and, because of what's going on in Thorwald's apartment—the more interesting movie, as it were—Jefferies doesn't, until the very last minute, decide that he needs to call the police. He takes action but, given that the woman has already pulled out the sleeping pills and pulled down the blinds—symbolically, the curtains are about to end on her story—he may be doing so too late.

An interconnection between two of the stories going on behind the windows is established here. Mrs. Lonelyheart hears the pianist and his jazz ensemble playing in the apartment above. The music lifts her and pulls her out of her suicidal spiral.

Since he is already on the phone, Jefferies is able to call the police for assistance when he sees that Thorwald is about to attack Lisa in Thorwald's apartment. At this point, Hitchcock becomes Hitchcock at his darkest. The audience already cares about these characters. They seem like real people, even though they've only been glimpsed through lenses at this point, and the following sequences are incredibly tense.

Hitchcock Reminds You to Fear Him

Lisa has made the ill-advised but very courageous move to get into Thorwald's apartment and look for clues they cannot see through the binoculars. Thorwald has been persuaded to leave his apartment by Lisa's delivery of a note that implies that someone knows he killed his wife. Jefferies has set him up, giving Lisa, Stella and Jefferies approximately 15 minutes—they believe—to get what they need to out Thorwald for the murderer he is. The clock is set and the countdown begins.

Thorwald makes it home and confronts Lisa. The confrontation quickly turns violent and, making everything even worse, Thorwald turns out the light.

Stewart is incredible in this sequence. The agony he goes through at not being able to do anything is palpable. He has, to this point, been the passive observer and has been able to watch what goes on in his neighbor's lives—even the murderous things—without having to put himself at any real risk. Now, through Lisa, he is at risk. He also seems to realize how much he cares about her in this moment.

Lisa, being as smart as she is, takes advantage of what would seem to be a bad situation for anyone. The police arrive and break up the fight, with Lisa getting arrested for breaking into Thorwald's house. She plays it up, shows Jefferies that she has the wedding ring by flashing it on her finger through the window and is taken to safety by the police.

Things just got worse for Jefferies, however, as Thorwald realized what Lisa was doing and, for the first time and in the worst way possible, Jefferies is busted by one of the people he's spying on.

When Hitchcock goes dark, he goes pitch black. He does so metaphorically, of course, but also literally in this case. Jefferies kills the lights after telling Stella to get out of the apartment to get help. In his dark apartment, he picks up the only weapon he has: his camera flash. Ironically enough, the equipment that he used to enable him to be a passive observer now serves as his only protection against a very real, and deadly, threat.

Thorwald takes it a step further, killing the lights in the hallway as he noisily approaches Jefferies' door. The sound of his footsteps, and the sheer mass they imply, only make the situation more tense. Jefferies is in a wheelchair, quite incapable of fighting back and is facing a man who likely would have been able to kill him barehanded if Jefferies were fully mobile and healthy.

Jefferies uses the flash to blind Thorwald several times as the hulking murderer approaches across the apartment. It works for a brief second each time, but Thorwald is not so easily dissuaded.

He gets ahold of Jefferies and ends up dragging him to the edge of the fire escape, where Jefferies only manages to hold on by his fingertips. The police hear the commotion and manage to subdue Thorwald, but not before Jefferies plunges from the window. A lesser filmmaker may have done the classic "Grab my hand!" trope at this point, but Hitchcock wants you to know that the danger is real. In Hitchcock's world, violence is always very real. It doesn't take a machete or a glove made out of knives to make a killer. It just takes some determination, a bit of physical presence and the willingness to toss someone off a high perch.

Jefferies hits the ground, but he lives, and Stella and Lisa are there to make sure he's okay. The police have found evidence that precisely confirms Jefferies' suspicions and Thorwald is about to take the police on a "tour of the East River."

After the climax, the aforementioned scene of Lisa reclining on the bed while Jefferies sits in a chair, now sporting two casts, sets things back to normal.

Why This Film Works

The woman who made the speech about being a good neighbor after her dog was killed by Thorwald was right. The jazz musician saved the suicidal Mrs. Lonelyheart; the woman herself has a new puppy, carrying new promise for happiness; Miss Torso greets her comically undersized soldier boyfriend as he comes home from the service, adding a bit of joy to her apparently boring life.

In the end, Hitchcock presents a challenge to the viewer in the midst of one of the most entertaining thrillers of the era, perhaps ever. Voyeurism can be entertaining and, in fact, thrilling, under the right circumstances, but human beings actually engaging with one another is what removes much of the menace from the world. Sometimes, it's too easy to get caught up watching dramas in which the viewer isn't even involved and forget what we have right in front of us, whether they're on a screen or through a neighbor's windows.

While the modern world may make it seem like we are all entirely detached from one another, watching dramas from a remote, safe location while they unfold for people we don't even interact with personally, the most satisfying parts of life are when people engage, help one another and take risks to make sure that the world isn't too dangerous a place for anyone.

One other element in the film that's hard to miss is the parallel between Jefferies and Mrs. Thorwald. Like Jefferies, Mrs. Thorwald was bedridden and was victimized because she was surrounded by people who were, in the deadliest way, evil. Jefferies lives because, in the same situation, he is surrounded by people who genuinely care for him and even love him, and that proves to be his salvation—tangible connections to the right people.

http://www.rogerebert.com/reviews/great-movie-rear-window-1954

http://dramatica.com/analysis/rear-window

Bonus Chapter

The Yellow Wallpaper: You're Not Crazy? We Can Fix That!

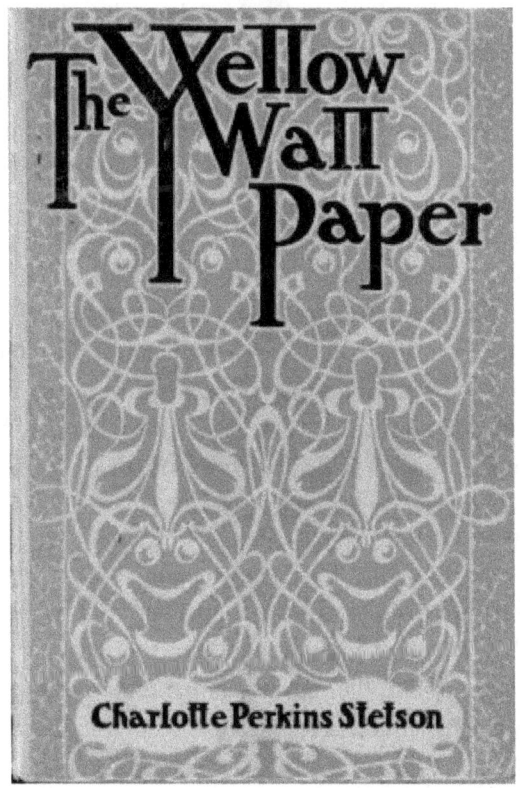

Cover for Charlotte Perkins Gillman's short story about mental health.

In 1892, Charlotte Perkins Gilman published a story in *New England Magazine* entitled *The Yellow Wallpaper*. It has many of the hallmarks of the thriller films that would come along in the 20th century in terms of how it deals with the topic of insanity. Specifically, this story is about a woman who is quite sane at the beginning of her ordeal, as described in the book, but ends up having gone mad by the end. Through it all, the people to whom she tries to reach out ignore her, even as they try to treat a fictional illness from which they believe she suffers.

The Plot

The plot of *The Yellow Wallpaper* hinges on the Resting Cure or the Rest Cure, a method of psychological 'treatment' that was in vogue during the 19th century. At that time, it was generally held by medical professionals that women were prone to hysteria and that, by removing from them all access to any sort of stimulation, they could recover. The Resting Cure, in practice, was similar to solitary confinement as it is practiced in prisons—as a punishment—today.

The narrator in this story is locked in the upstairs room of a mansion. Her husband is the villain, as it were, of this story, as it is his belief that his wife needs this treatment. She has recently given birth and has started to show hysterical tendencies. In plain English, this diagnosis of hysteria was oftentimes pinned on women who expressed dissatisfaction with their lives, depression or just about any other mental hardship that made them difficult to deal with, as far as their husbands and others were concerned.

One of the opening lines clearly illustrates how the narrator's complaints are dismissed by her husband. Saying that the "ancestral halls" that they have rented out for the summer have something strange about them, the narrator laments in the opening lines: "John laughs at me, of course, but one expects that in marriage."

The narrator's husband happens to be a physician, so between his qualifications and her being a woman, there is little she can do to plead her case. The narrator, in fact, believes that her malaise would best be treated with a bit of distraction, perhaps even some healthy work—something with which many modern psychologists would likely agree quite readily.

Nonetheless, the narrator finds herself confined to an upstairs room. It is a dingy room, with scratched floorboards and yellow wallpaper with a busy pattern. That latter decoration will become integral to the progression of the story.

The Descent

In thriller films, it's not uncommon to have the protagonist or antagonist descend into madness and to use that as a device to advance the plot. In *Memento*, for instance, the protagonist has a mental condition that makes his life confusing at best and deadly at worst. At the end of the film, it is revealed that he has found ways to manipulate his own form of madness—which is actually amnesia in this case, but which involves some willful disassociation from the actual events of his life. In *Psycho*, the antagonist is quite mad by the time the audience meets him, but the audience explores his madness as the film progresses. *Silence of the Lambs*, of course, centers on various forms of madness as a main element of its plot.

The movie that comes closest to referencing this story, at least among those featured in this book, is the 1944 film *Gaslight*, which very much involves a similar and equally chilling premise as *The Yellow Wallpaper*.

In *The Yellow Wallpaper*, the narrator has a bad feeling about the house that could indicate that she is, indeed, suffering from some anxiety. Every protest the woman raises about the home and her treatment, however, is dismissed as an instance of her manifesting the hysteria for which her husband intends to treat her.

The narrator's entire day is dictated by her husband. Even though she tries her best to go along with his direction, she starts to become understandably restless. The windows in the room in which she's kept are barred. There is a gate preventing her from going down the stairs and she's confined against her will. In modern times, this would likely be regarded as false imprisonment, as her freedom is completely taken away from her.

She obsesses over the wallpaper, asks to have it changed at one point, but, like everything else she has an opinion about, her irritation with the dingy, busy wallpaper is ignored. The wallpaper itself becomes an obsession of hers, and she begins to think of it as having some will of its own: "This paper looks to me as if it knew what a vicious influence it had!" she laments.

Gradually, the narrator begins to see faces in the wallpaper. Eventually, she begins to see a woman within it. She believes the woman is moving the pattern on the wallpaper by asking it and, eventually, she believes that there is more than one woman behind the wallpaper. The narrator believes the woman she focuses on the most is trying to climb through the paper itself.

The narrator's hallucinations become more severe. She sees the woman from the wallpaper everywhere, creeping around outside the home through every window that the narrator gazes through. The hallucinations become worse at night. Her writings become more disjointed, nonsensical and obsessed with the wallpaper and the woman she sees creeping around behind its front pattern.

By the end of the story, the protagonist has utterly snapped. She's become convinced that she had to free the woman from behind the wallpaper and has peeled it off from the walls. Her husband manages to get into the room after she's locked herself in, refusing to leave, and finds her creeping around the perimeter of the room, touching the wall with her shoulder so that she doesn't become lost.

In the end, she is broken, though it's likely that she initially only suffered from a minor case of post-partum depression or, perhaps, was simply a little discontent with her life.

How the Trope Plays Out Today

The Yellow Wallpaper utilizes a trope that TVTropes refers to as the Mind Screw. It's basically exactly what the name implies. The story employs elements that leave the reader confused as to what actually happened. This, of course, is readily seen used in the film *Memento*, which confuses the audience as to what is going on in the story with reverse-time storytelling and other devices.

Another element of this trope that is clearly seen in some thrillers is the reveal of small twists and surprises on which the audience depends to understand the film at all. For instance, using *Memento* once again, it's not apparent why the protagonist leaves himself sometimes-cryptic clues when he could just write down the entire narrative of what happened the day before, eliminating altogether the need for him to investigate a mystery over and over again. As it turns out, that is exactly his point.

Jacob's Ladder uses similar methods of storytelling. Much of what takes place in the film makes no sense until the final reveal and, at that point, everything makes perfect sense. Like the narrator in *The Yellow Wallpaper*, Jacob Singer is being driven mad by dangerously misguided psychological practices, though his situation resolves much differently than that of the protagonist in *The Yellow Wallpaper*.

The unreliable narrator is also a common trope used in thriller films and it's used to great effect in *The Yellow Wallpaper*. In this book, the narrator's descent into madness is documented in her writings, though the reader cannot be certain whether she was mad from the start or not, which gives the story an element of tension.

The Yellow Wallpaper was made into a film in 2011, which diverges significantly from the original story. If one happens to be a true fan of thrillers, particularly ones that deal with themes of insanity, isolation and victimization by misguided authority figures, *The Yellow Wallpaper* makes for a great read. It's particularly good after having watched any thriller in which the protagonist is manipulated psychologically by nefarious characters, such as *Gaslight*.

In fact, *Gaslight* has much in common with *The Yellow Wallpaper*. Both stories take place in houses that are menacing in and of themselves. Both evoke sympathy in the reader/viewer by showing the madness that the protagonist is suffering. Unlike *The Yellow*

Wallpaper, however, *Gaslight* has what amounts to a happy ending. *The Yellow Wallpaper* may not fit neatly into what would be considered a thriller today, but its themes of falling into madness are certainly ones that have been explored to a great degree by thriller filmmakers and, in many instances, that have proven very successful at making the audience sympathize with and be very afraid for the protagonist.

This story is in the public domain and can be read online at many different sites. It's also available in printed form from numerous different publishers and has become a favorite of those who engage in literary analysis.

http://www.library.csi.cuny.edu/dept/history/lavender/wallpaper.html

http://tvtropes.org/pmwiki/pmwiki.php/Main/MindScrew

North by Northwest: The Perfect Spy Thriller (1959)
Director: Alfred Hitchcock

Starring: Cary Grant

        Eva Marie Saint

        James Mason

        Jessie Royce Landis

"...I got into it by accident..."

-Roger Thornhill, *North by Northwest*

For those who grew up on James Bond, some of the possibilities inherent in the spy thriller genre may be lost on them. A spy thriller can be, at once, murkier, more complex and, in many regards, more exciting than the action/thriller/spy flick formula that is so popular—and, in fact, the norm—today.

One needs look no further than the work of the master, Alfred Hitchcock, to confirm this. *North by Northwest* is widely considered to be among the best spy films ever made and, in fact, many consider it the perfect spy thriller. The plot is complex and there are real rewards for the viewer following it through to the end. Cary Grant is excellent in the lead role, as is the entire cast in their roles. Being a Hitchcock film, *North by Northwest* serves up twist after twist, the direction is flawless and the entire affair is still a joy to watch.

Delving into the film, it's notable that, with very little violence and certainly not at all extreme portrayals of violence when it does occur, this film still delivers in terms of thrills.

A Brilliant Setup for a Brilliant Film

Roger O. Thornhill (Cary Grant) is a man who is accustomed to being able to handle things. In the first scenes in *North by Northwest*, we see him walking with his secretary, giving her instructions on how to handle a variety of different tasks. He always knows what to do. He rattles off instructions in a rapid staccato, never pausing for a moment, no matter what she might need him to take care of. Confronted with the hustle involved with getting a cab in New York, he expertly lies his way into an open cab, saying that his secretary is ill.

No matter what he needs to deal with, Roger Thornhill is accustomed to knowing the right answer for any question put to him. All of that is about to change drastically and Thornhill's world is about to be turned upside down, inside out and to become much more challenging than he ever wanted.

The setup is perfect for this film. We first see Thornhill truly in his element, amidst the chaos of New York City yet managing to keep in control of everything. He makes it apparent that, as an advertising executive, he's aware that his job is really about lying and, as one would expect, that will become very important as the plot unfolds. Thornhill is not a liar because he is malicious. He's a liar because it is his job and because it allows him to sell the products that he's paid to bring to market. It's just part of his job and he's fine with it, even a bit proud of how good at it he is.

Thornhill's life is unfolding according to his plans and expectations, by every indication, and he heads off to an exclusive club to have a business meeting—including martinis, of course, as this is the 1950s, after all—with some equally slick associates. This is the last normal thing that Roger Thornhill will do for some time and, in fact, the last time that he will feel truly in control of his life, as he's accustomed to being.

The first inklings that things are about to change for Thornhill are not subtle. He ends up being abducted by a pair of heavies, one of whom sticks a gun in Thornhill's ribs as they roughly escort him out of the club, one of the thugs pointing out to him that the gun is pointed at his heart. Thornhill immediately—and really with impressive calm—pulls out his usual tricks, fast-talking and trying his charm on the thugs. He maintains, honestly, that he has no idea what's going on and tries to make an escape from the sedan he's being spirited away in, finding the door locked, of course.

From there, Thornhill's ordeal really begins. He is taken to an opulent mansion by a man he believes to be named Townsend. The man, however, is actually Phillip Vandamm, a spy who is behind Thornhill's abduction. Vandamm obviously has mistaken Thornhill for someone else—George Kaplan—and believes Thornhill to be acting a part. He orders one of his heavies, Leonard, to dispatch Thornhill, which they plan to do by getting him drunk to the point of passing out, putting him in a sports car and sending him careening off of a cliff.

Thornhill, 1950s businessman that he is, can handle his liquor and manages to drive away before eventually crashing and being arrested for drunken driving.

He relates his story honestly to the police but, given that Townsend is not at the mansion and that the story is rather fantastical, the authorities decide to investigate to figure out whether or not Thornhill is lying, which they assume he must be.

Townsend turns out to be a diplomat at the United Nations. Thornhill decides to go visit the man at the UN, a decision that turns out to be disastrous. Valerian, one of the henchmen who originally abducted Thornhill, expertly throws a knife into Townsend's back. Thornhill catches Townsend as he falls, inadvertently pulling out the knife and ending up standing above the dead man, looking like a dagger-wielding assassin to everyone, including the newspaper reporter who snaps a photo of poor Thornhill with the bloody knife in his hand.

Thornhill is now a wanted murderer and he has to run.

By this point, it's apparent that the audience is in for a ride and Hitchcock does a great job of communicating the chaos of the situation with his direction. Thornhill doesn't know what's going on, but he knows he has to make a break for it, as even the most open-minded investigator would have a hard time believing that he didn't stab the diplomat in the back. Even a fibber as accomplished as Thornhill would have a tough time of it selling his story to the police, given the preponderance of evidence that indicates his guilt.

Things are only going to get more complicated for Thornhill.

Why This Setup Works

Cary Grant was a rather popular leading man at the time that *North by Northwest* was filmed. He had a very cultured manner about him and spoke in the smooth accent characteristic of people with both British and American backgrounds. He had no difficulty communicating charm, wit and charisma, but he was, at least by the standards one would expect for a spy, not particularly well-suited.

Grant's demeanor came off as that of a ladies' man. He was a charmer, to be sure, but, at least in *North by Northwest*, he doesn't have the demeanor that your usual spy movie thriller protagonist would have. He doesn't come off as deadly, deceitful in any dangerous way and certainly doesn't come off as someone who is accustomed to being on the run.

This makes *North by Northwest* work. To believe the premise, one has to first believe that Thornhill is truly a fish out of water. As the film progresses, he becomes more and more effective and we see him demonstrate that some of his skills are actually quite well-suited to the life he's been thrust into, but overall, he's outmatched, barely able to keep ahead of the people who want him dead and mostly confused by what's going on. Grant plays this role brilliantly, coming off as someone who one would probably love to go out for a drink with, but if he were to go off on a story about the time he was caught up in a murderous caper involving international espionage, one would probably assume he was just fibbing. After all, this guy wouldn't last a moment if pitted against trained, professional and ruthless killers.

Or would he?

The Plot Thickens

Thornhill is about to go on an adventure. As Matthew Pickle points out, Hitchcock made a point of grounding the audience at each location where Thornhill ends up with a strong establishing shot. Thornhill does end up, by the end of the film, travelling to the UN, to an Indiana cornfield, to Chicago and, eventually, to Mount Rushmore, in addition to other places in between. As the character winds his way through the film and these various landscapes, he also evolves as a person. Each new stop along the journey sees Thornhill becoming more adept at surviving and, in an odd fashion, more comfortable with being thrown into a situation that started with a case of mistaken identity.

Thornhill, after basically setting himself up as the murderer of a diplomat, escapes by train. He gets on the 20th Century Limited and this is the first time we see the woman who will provide the romantic interest for the film, Eva Marie Saint playing Eve Kendall.

Kendall helps Thornhill to evade the police searching the train for him. Their interactions are full of plenty of 1950s era double entendre and what today would certainly be considered sexual harassment. After all, what modern man would sit down with a woman he barely knows and tell her he just can't help but think about making love to her? It all proves to be a ruse, of course. Kendall happens to be working for the spies pursuing him. She slips a note to Vandamm, asking what she's supposed to do with Thornhill.

Thornhill still doesn't know who Kaplan, the man he's been mistaken for, actually is. Kendall tells him, once they reach Chicago, that she's going to meet with Kaplan. She helps Thornhill to escape by bribing a railroad worker to give Thornhill his clothes. Thornhill manages to slip by the police, carrying Kendall's luggage, and slips into a bathroom, where his face full of shaving cream allows him to avoid being identified by the people searching for him.

The Plane Scene

If there is one scene in this movie that people who haven't seen it might be familiar with, it is the one from which the iconic image of Cary Grant running away from an airplane is taken. This scene is Hitchcock at his best.

Thornhill ends up in the middle of farm country in Indiana. The landscape is empty, a vast plain with mostly harvested cornfields. He waits at an intersection for Kaplan to show up, but every car just passes him by. One man stops and catches a bus, which Thornhill opts to pass on, which sets up the scene.

A crop duster is plying the air in the background of the scene, the only object of note in the bleak landscape. There is no one around and the man getting on the bus points out that the crop duster is dusting where there aren't even any crops to dust.

The shark is in the water or, as it happens, the air.

The plane comes toward Thornhill, missing him by mere feet as it passes overhead. The next passes reveal that the plane is equipped with a machine gun and, in a rather clever use of chemical warfare, the pilot dumps a load of dust on Thornhill to flush him out of a patch of standing corn in which he's hiding.

This scene is so well remembered simply because of the tension involved. If Thornhill were James Bond, a combination of unusual athleticism, probably some sort of gadget and a lot of training would have reduced the plane to a minor threat that needed to be done away with. In Thornhill's case, the plane is a threat that is way out of his league and he only manages to escape it through luck and desperate action.

This sequence alone makes *North by Northwest* worth watching. Grant's terror is palpable and the scene has a marvelous simplicity to it, especially given the location; it forces the viewer to fully engage with the protagonist and the pilot who's determined to put him in the ground.

We're All Roger Thornhill

While the eventual climax of the film is reached through a very steady and masterful ratcheting up of tension from Hitchcock, the real thrill in this film is, in part, watching Thornhill evolve. This is what makes this film a perfect spy thriller.

While the *007* and *Bourne* franchises certainly serve up plenty of thrills, there is more of a suspension of disbelief involved. After all, it seems as if James Bond is very lucky in constantly running across hit men who are just slightly outmatched enough to allow Bond to escape over and over again. The audience watching those types of films is also identifying with an elite secret agent who, in reality, is not a realistic character to identify with. Those films are more based in fantasy, allowing the audience to pretend that they just might have been that elite secret agent if things had been slightly different.

Thornhill could be any of us. He has no idea about the world of espionage. He does learn, throughout the film, to be very clever at surviving and even becomes a willing participant in the game, risking his life to save Kendall, who turns out to be on the right side after all.

He negotiates double and triple crosses, makes daring escapes and barely survives a quite thrilling encounter with the villains on Mount Rushmore at the climax of the film.

This film works because Roger Thornhill is believable. He doesn't turn out to be a master of spy craft who just didn't know it, but he's smarter than average and that's enough. He might be something of a con, but he is completely put off by the level of deceit that the spymaster he eventually encounters demonstrates. He is not made for the world into which he was thrust and this is apparent at every turn.

North by Northwest is worth watching in part because of the reality of the situation portrayed, which is an unusual thing to say for a spy thriller. The film involves a character who could be any of us. The violence isn't over the top—particularly by modern standards—but the fact that Thornhill is dealing with deadly people is made readily apparent. There is enough comic relief to make the tension bearable and the comic relief never crosses the line into being cheesy or trite.

This is a sophisticated film for sophisticated viewers and, more than anything else, it's a great ride. After it's over, you'll be glad that you and Roger Thornhill were bundled into a car at gunpoint, as it began an adventure that allowed a man who had had two marriages break up because he led too dull a life to transform himself into a capable and admirable hero who demonstrates courage and wit at every turn, even when he doesn't quite know what's going on.

http://matthewpickle.wordpress.com/2011/01/27/north-by-northwest-film-analysis/

Bonus Chapter: Who was Hitchcock?

Alfred Hitchcock is probably more associated with the thriller genre than any other person. There have been television shows and magazines that center on this genre that were branded with his name. He's also renowned as one of the greatest directors of all times and his films, almost across the board, receive high praise. What was it about this man that led him to be so associated with one particular genre of film? There are endless debates about that, but there are some things about the man that clearly feed into the name he made for himself.

Hitchcock's Background

Hitchcock was born in 1899. This places him in what is usually referred to as the Lost Generation, the generation that was of military service age during World War I. He grew up in England and suffered with lifelong obesity. He also had some incidents in his life that would affect him forever.

In one particular instance, when Hitchcock was very young, his father got mad at him and sent him down to the police department. He gave him a note that asked the officers to jail him for five minutes as punishment. This may seem a bit severe—and it certainly is, by any modern notion of parenting—and the effect it had was probably not what his father wanted. Hitchcock was fearful of the police for the rest of his life because of this.

Hitchcock had been working in film since the days of silent movies. His career started off very rocky, but by the 1950s, he had become something of a force in films and ended up making some of the most remembered and loved movies of all time. This is the period in which he made classics such as *North by Northwest* and *Rear Window*.

Each of these films shows some of the characteristics for which Hitchcock would become famous. They all have a very pronounced sense of the darkest humor to them. The characters oftentimes laugh in what really is the face of death, or manage to be lighthearted despite their predicaments, in some regards. Not all of his films are as dark as his reputation would indicate. *To Catch a Thief*, for example, is quite endearing in many regards and is more of an adventure than a thriller, though it does have thriller elements to it.

When Hitchcock does get dark, however, as we've seen in his films, he goes there full-force. *Psycho* is likely the best example of this. The film is still considered a horror classic today and actually embodies a great deal of why Hitchcock is so respected in how it was made. It's not a high-budget film, according to Thomas Leitch in *The Encyclopedia of Alfred Hitchcock*, proving that expensive sets and high-budget effects aren't necessary to elicit a good scare out of an audience. It's also very brutal in how violence is portrayed, showing it in very human terms rather than in the fantastical forms characteristic of horror, but is all the more horrific because of that.

A Complex Man

Some directors have reputations that are not altogether good in terms of their interpersonal skills and how they treat their actors. Kubrick is one example; Hitchcock is another.

When he was filming *The 39 Steps*, he referred to one actress as a tart regularly. He fairly terrorized some of his actresses and did not have a reputation as an easy man to work with. Like many of his characters, he was flawed, but he was very good at what he did for a living. His body of work serves to make that very apparent.

Style

Hitchcock's style had some remarkable elements that make it stand out from that of most other filmmakers and, in fact, that have had profound influences on filmmaking over the years.

He used a voyeuristic camera technique, for which he is quite renowned, that draws the audience into the film. It's a first-person point-of-view technique that is used heavily, for instance, in the film *Rear Window*.

He also used what he called the MacGuffin. This technique involves setting up the plot by using details that are never fully revealed to the audience. For instance, in *Rear Window*, we never actually see the murder, the body parts being removed from the home or most anything else that goes on at Thorwald's apartment. Even though we don't see those details, they drive most of the plot in the film. This technique is very much associated with Hitchcock. Watching for it can be an amusing way to take in his films. There are plenty of details that are left unexplained, and that makes his films even more interesting than they are on the surface.

The Average Guy

Many of Hitchcock's characters are not up to the challenges with which they are presented. In fact, until they overcome those challenges, many of his characters are completely ordinary. Thornhill in *North by Northwest*, for instance, is a very slick customer, but he's no international spy and the movie makes that apparent.

This is one of the appeals of Hitchcock's films and, in fact, one of the things that gives many thrillers their overall appeal. The audience can sympathize with the character because, in fact, any audience member could probably be that character. This is not always true, however. In *Rear Window*, the protagonist is an accomplished and adventurous photographer with a renowned dressmaker for a fiancée. In *To Catch a Thief*, the protagonist is a very distinguished, but retired, jewel thief.

Why They Endure

There are endless books on Hitchcock and his importance. What really makes his films so effective, in part, is the quality.

His shots are flawless. The pacing in his films is almost always perfect. When he's funny and lighthearted, the fun is enjoyable, not childish or contrived. When he's dark, you will be afraid.

Hitchcock's films are classics, but they're also as engaging as any contemporary films. The viewer need not apologize for the films because they are products of their time to enjoy them. They are timeless in many regards, and their characters tend to be very human, which makes them work in any era.

For any thriller fan, a Hitchcock library is a necessity. For anyone interested in exploring thrillers more, his films, particularly those from the 1950s and 1960s, are always good places to start.

After all these years, the shower scene in *Psycho* will still make you jump in terror, even in an era when thrillers and horror films are much harsher than they were in Hitchcock's day.

http://www.labyrinth.net.au/~muffin/faqs_c.html#Answer%201

Fatal Attraction: Sexual Paranoia in the Age of AIDS (1987)

Director: Adrian Lyne

Starring: Michael Douglas

Glenn Close

Anne Archer

Thrillers and other film genres sometimes use the antagonist as an enforcer of traditional morality. *Fatal Attraction* is a fine example of this. The film involves a rather common premise: a married man has an affair and it comes back to haunt him. This is a very effective psychological thriller, however, particularly because of Close's portrayal of Alex Forrest, a woman you should never, ever mislead.

The Plot and Setup

Dan Gallagher has a pretty great life. He has a wife who loves him, Beth, and a 6-year-old daughter. He's an attorney, does well for himself and calls New York home. There's really nothing wrong with his life, but he decides to make a mess of it anyway.

At a party, he meets Alex Forrest. Alex immediately takes an interest in Dan and, before too long, he gets an opportunity to take their interactions one step further. While his wife and daughter are away, Dan succumbs to his baser urges and starts an affair with Alex. Their sex involves everything up to and including the kitchen sink and, in fact, it's almost comical. Things get very dark very quickly, however, and if the overblown movie sex puts you off guard, you'll pay for it soon enough.

Alex doesn't like being ignored and, after she becomes too forward and starts to present a real threat to his perfect life, Dan tries just that. He rebuffs her and, pretty soon, the late-night calls kick off the terror she subjects him and his family to. Somewhat predictably, but still effective in terms of making the plot more involving, she lets him know that he got her pregnant.

Alex begins a reign of terror on Dan's life. Of course, his wife finds out what happened eventually, putting his marriage at risk. His daughter is thrust into peril, his wife is injured in a car accident, the family's pet rabbit gets boiled to death and a deadly confrontation ensues.

This film follows a very predictable pattern in some ways, but it's Alex's madness and the moral ambiguity of the main character that really make it something unique. *Fatal Attraction* has a lot to offer that a plot summary just doesn't illustrate and, to understand this movie, one has to delve deeper.

The Age of AIDS

In the 1980s, the United States and the world were still reeling at the revelation that AIDS was, at the time, an incurable, largely untreatable, rapidly spreading and not well-understood disease that was oftentimes spread sexually. It was already known outside the US, having been identified as early as the 1950s. It was not until the early 1980s, however, that it became a recognized killer in the US,.

The sexual escapades that Dan and Alex engage in are very liberated, to say the least. The consequences of this type of sex are oftentimes portrayed as deadly, particularly in horror films, but there are plenty of thrillers that use this trope. *Basic Instinct* is another good example of how the link between carnal pleasures and death is portrayed in films.

The immorality in this film doesn't involve lying to Alex. Dan tells her flat-out that he doesn't want to end his marriage and that he just wants to have a sexual encounter with her. She obliges, but it's not just a sexual encounter. It is, in every way, a trap.

There is a theme of seemingly fun and harmless sex having consequences in this film. There is also a sense that, at some level, the man who instigated all of this deserved it.

Alex can be seen as something of a victim, but Dan did tell her, after all. She was being given an opportunity to make an informed decision as an adult and, of course, she opted for what traditional morality would hold was the immoral choice. While Dan ends up paying the price for his infidelity, so does Alex. This is a woman on the verge of a breakdown and Dan's fling with her provides the little push she needs to go right off the cliff.

Alex doesn't end up giving Dan a sexually transmitted disease. If that had happened, it would have changed the entire nature of the film. What she does end up doing is become overly attached to him and, later, we see that there is some justification for this, given that she is pregnant. Alex has no choice and is trapped by the consequences of his actions. Were she reasonable and sane, Dan would have to deal with her pregnancy, regardless of how badly he wanted to avoid telling his wife he had an affair. Given that Alex is completely unreasonable, he would have had to deal with the consequences of his affair even if she wasn't pregnant, which makes infidelity and sexual immorality something with inescapable consequences for the characters in this film.

At the time, AIDS in the US was principally associated with homosexual men, as most of the earliest cases affected that population. This allowed the disease to be cast in a way that associated it with what was perceived to be immoral at the time, as the gay rights movement hadn't yet gotten much traction. It was also associated with promiscuous behavior and drug use, both of which fell outside of the range of traditional morality as it was understood at the time. This made it difficult to discuss the disease objectively and led to a great deal of discrimination against sufferers.

The action in *Fatal Attraction* provides something of a mirror of this period in terms of societal struggles with redefining sexual morality. While Alex and Dan are in a situation that involves some rather conventional elements—cheating, accidental pregnancy—the situation also involves the deadly consequences of sex and that is, perhaps, why this film got so much attention at the time. It's a sort of desublimation, allowing for a frank discussion of whether adults who make sexual decisions outside the perceived norms deserve some sort of punishment or if there are, in fact, tragic situations that don't emanate from human failings and weakness but that, instead, emanate from common human behaviors and urges.

Safe sex was the go-to phrase in those days. What Dan ended up having was very, very unsafe sex.

You Cannot Make this Go Away

HIV, the virus that causes AIDS, cannot be gotten rid of once it is contracted. Death was inevitable for HIV-positive individuals in the 1980s. At that time, provided they didn't survive long enough to take advantage of the better treatments that came about in the following decades, anyone with HIV was going to die of AIDS—eventually.

Alex Forrest's insanity, in some ways, serves as a symbolic representation of this. She is not going to go away, either, and you're either going to live with that or get killed. This character, like a disease, becomes worse and worse as the story unfolds. Dan may have brought this menace into the house, but soon enough it spreads and affects his family as well.

Alex starts by simply interrupting Dan's life. She calls at all hours. They get a new phone; they move. She finds out where they went. Alex is not only akin to a disease in that she cannot be fled, she is also a symbol of guilt. Her fury, in fact, acts in the story much as did the Furies of ancient myth. She is a punishment for wrongs done. She is an embodiment of the guilt that Dan deserves to feel, as he has lied and broken his wedding vows to a woman who is, in every regard, a great partner deserving of more respect and honesty. Alex is his conscience come to life, and until he deals with it, it's not going to get any better.

When It Gets Dark It Gets Very Dark

Alex seems almost manageable until she tells Dan that she's pregnant. Now, she's absolutely not going away. Dan makes the biggest mistake of all in how he addresses that.

Alex clearly wants more of a connection to Dan. She wants him to love her, basically. He doesn't, but now she has something that ensures that he can't just ignore her. She's carrying his child. Dan offers to help with an abortion. Not only has he betrayed her, he's now offering to help take away from her the only way she has to keep him on the hook, and she goes off the rails completely afterward.

This sets up the escalation of the stalking scenario and the violence that follows. Alex finds where the Gallaghers have moved to and comes after them again. There's already reason to be afraid of this woman. In a scene where Dan starts to beat her, she nearly kills him with a knife. Dan is a liar and riddled with guilt and, clearly, he's bitten off more than he can chew. He can't handle this woman emotionally, he can't have her in his life and she's a genuine physical threat to him.

Alex begins to assault every part of his life. She kidnaps his daughter, kills their pet in one of the cruelest ways possible—and a symbolic one; the rabbit is dead, which used to be a metaphor for saying someone is pregnant due to the test administered at the time—and eventually invades his home and assaults his family.

The ending scene of this movie is one of the most remembered in cinematic history. It gripped audiences in a way that few films have and had enough tension to make Hitchcock proud.

The Climax You Won't Forget

The audience has already been set up for some terrifying scenes at the point that the movie crashes to its climax. The scene where Beth discovers the rabbit is particularly effective in setting up the tension. She edges closer and closer to the stove, ultimately being horrified and discovering that things are much worse than she suspected. This incident eventually persuades Dan to tell her about the fact that he cheated on her and that he had an affair. Obviously, given what has happened, Beth knows that they're dealing with a disordered personality.

Dan has already gone violent by this point over the abduction of their daughter, and the audience already knows that Alex is very, very dangerous. The pieces are all in place.

Beth is drawing a bath when Alex appears and attacks her with a kitchen knife. The two struggle, getting Dan's attention as he's making a pot of tea, which has just come to a boil. Again, not too subtle.

He races up to the bathroom and goes after Alex. At this point, Alex has gone from a woman who embodies an awful mistake Dan made to a deadly and immediate threat to his family. Dan overpowers her, pushing her into the bathtub and, apparently, drowning her. This is where the film gets one of its most effective jump scares.

Alex does the jumping. She emerges from the tub, brandishing her knife and, just as she's transformed from a jilted—and insane—woman to a full-fledged movie monster, Beth comes in and shoots her through the heart, finally killing her. Once again, there are ample opportunities to see symbolism in this. Alex gets shot through the heart.

Why This Film Works

There is no victory in the end of this film. Presumably, Dan was not only forced to kill a woman whose insanity he is somewhat guilty of bringing about, he also killed his own child in the process.

The film doesn't end on a happy note. In fact, it's become iconic for the terror it elicits in audiences, for the incredibly creepy performance that Close gives and for the ambiguity that surrounds the main character. Did he deserve this? No. No one deserves to be terrorized in that way. Was Alex deceived? Arguably, though she was aware that Dan was just looking for a good time. Did Dan put his family in danger—and probably break it up—because of a moment of weakness? Yes. Inarguably, yes, in fact, and this is where the discomfort in this movie largely emanates from.

Did Alex get what she deserved? Legally, of course, yes, as people have the right to defend themselves. Did she deserve to be such a broken person? Who knows?

Fatal Attraction works because it does, to a great degree, reflect a lot of the moral debates around sexuality and its consequences at the time. In the end, there are no easy answers and, sometimes, it's really only the human tragedy that's left in the wake of one bad decision or one instance of succumbing to a simple human urge.

http://www.avert.org/history-hiv-aids-us.htm

Jacob's Ladder: Terror, Madness and Conspiracy (1990)

Director: Adrian Lyne

Starring: Tim Robbins

Elizabeth Pena

Danny Aiello

Warning: This contains spoilers that will ruin this movie for those who haven't seen it. Watch the movie before reading.

Jacob Singer (Tim Robbins) is a character that embodies many of the very compassion-inducing difficulties that affect those who have served in wartime. He presumably suffers from PTSD and is plagued by flashback hallucinations that are, when they're not simply terrifying, utterly bizarre. He's tormented by the sense that he's losing his mind, but he's not even certain how or why it's all happening. This is the basic setup for *Jacob's Ladder*, a 1990 horror/psychological thriller that delivers in terms of tension, suspense, sheer terror and a twist ending that most first-time viewers will have a very hard time forgetting. This film offers a vision of one man's hell that is not easy to watch and that is certainly not easy to erase from one's mind once one has plunged deep into that rabbit hole with the protagonist.

This film is also notable for launching some of the most ferocious debates on the Internet as to the ultimate meaning of the film, what actually happens and why it all unfolds the way that it does. If you're in the mood for a movie that has it all for the psychological thriller/horror and conspiracy film fan, this is one that should definitely make its way into your player.

Supernatural Thriller

There are elements of *Jacob's Ladder* that make it easy to confuse this film with a supernatural thriller. It is actually a psychological thriller. This is most obviously observed in that what Singer sees is adequately explained by the workings of a fractured mind. There may be events that seem supernatural and various theological themes are referenced throughout the film, but this is, at its core, a film about a human being yearning for normalcy and being torn apart by internal, rather than external, demons.

Conspiracy Thriller

Jacob's Ladder also has heavy elements of a conspiracy thriller. This drives much of the paranoia in the film, but the conspiracy is never really laid out in certain terms until the very end of the film and it is absolutely not what the viewer is likely to expect. This particular film takes the theme of being victimized by a conspiracy and makes it orders of magnitude worse than more conventional films.

The Plot

Jacob Singer is serving in Vietnam during the worst years of the war. The opening of this film will be familiar to anyone who has watched movies that center on that particular conflict. Despite the familiar nature of these scenes, they do not lack in power.

During those opening scenes, which take place in the Mekong Delta in 1971, Singer and his group of fellow soldiers are presumably deep in the jungle. The scene is oddly peaceful to begin with; orange, tropical sun, helicopters flying lazily over rivers and a group of soldiers relaxing between battles. They are worse for wear, feet injured and sore and obviously they're exhausted, but they joke around with one another and are clearly a close bunch.

Movement in the tree line sets off the action, with mortars exploding. One of the soldiers says "something is wrong" and they all suddenly seem to be confused or ill. It's not apparent what's going on, but a nightmare scenario ensues, with soldiers having seizures, acting bizarrely and the chaos of battle erupting all around them as a firefight breaks out.

This should all be familiar fare for anyone who enjoys war movies, but there's something uniquely sinister about it from the start. The viewer, however, is left to wonder—at once and throughout the rest of the film—if it's only the inherent darkness of war that taints those opening scenes or if there is something much worse lurking beneath the surface.

Singer takes a bayonet to the abdomen, falls down and wakes up years later, on a subway in New York, gripping his side. He clearly hasn't gotten free of his memories of the war. Among the first things he sees on the dingy, empty subway is a sign that warns of the "hell" that life becomes when one does drugs.

This film unsettles the viewer from the start and it doesn't get any more pleasant from there out. Jacob Singer is a genuinely likeable guy from the moment he's introduced. He's boyish-looking, wears rather nerdy, round glasses and seems like someone who would be a good neighbor and friend. It makes the unfolding of this movie even harder to take, simply because it's so easy to care about Singer.

The mood is set up well right from the start and continues in the way it is established throughout. It is dark, surreal and disturbing. There is a sense of loneliness and incongruity throughout the film. In a dismal and empty subway that looks like it's never been cleaned, a sign promises "ecstasy" from a beauty product.

Singer is trapped in the train station and, trying to find an alternate way out, is nearly run down by a subway train. This all sounds conventional, but in the execution, it's gripping and quite terrifying.

It is in this scene where we see the first of the demons that torment Jacob, or at least external incarnations of them. A faceless man waves from the train that nearly runs Singer down as it fades away into the darkness of the tunnel.

Singer is haunted. In one of the scenes early on, he is sharing pictures with his girlfriend when he happens across a portrait of his son. It sends him into a crying fit. It's a completely normal reaction for a parent who has lost a child, but it sets up the viewers to understand some of the sorrow that Singer carries around in his heart; the things he cannot let go, and that concept becomes vital to the unfolding of the film.

Singer complains of having trouble with his back, for which he visits a chiropractor, Louis, played by Danny Aiello. Louis attempts to treat Singer's pain and, as far as the physical pain goes, he seems to be successful. He's clearly a major part of Singer's life, as well, as the two share stories about Singer's ex-wife while Singer receives treatment.

Louis will become a sort of guide figure in the film, talking to Singer about love and life in general, telling him about the nature of hell and trying to relieve his suffering. In some scenes, there is a clear connection between the chiropractor and the flashbacks that Singer suffers, with Louis sometimes looking like an angel—as Jacob notes—in the scenes.

There are times in this film where there is real joy, which makes the film effective. Louis offers Jacob genuine comfort. Just before Singer is almost run down by a car driven by the faceless demons first seen on the subway, a group of women sing "Mr. Postman" to Singer flirtatiously. It's a genuinely human moment and an authentically joyful moment amidst what unfolds as an absolute nightmare.

Nothing gets better from there on out. Singer's apparent journey into madness defines the film. We are moved back and forth in time; we are moved across different time lines. Singer's deceased son turns up in some of them; older than he was when we know he dies. This is all interspersed with random flashbacks to Vietnam.

If there is a central theme to this film, it is built around pain, sorrow, madness and confusion. Nothing about this film makes sense, until the very end, when it turns out to be much more sorrowful than one could have expected.

Tapping Into Insanity in Thrillers

Insanity is a powerful theme in thrillers. In some movies, such as *Psycho*, insanity provides the source of terror. In other films, as in *Jacob's Ladder*, insanity provides the motivation for the audience to sympathize with the protagonist.

Singer feels like he's going insane. He has hallucinations. He's apparently suffering from PTSD and sometimes exhibits the explosive rage characteristic of that disorder. He goes to his doctor, whom he maintains he's been seeing for years, and finds out that there is no record of him ever being treated by the doctor. He later finds out that the doctor died in a car explosion and the person who gives this explanation is vague and evasive in a way that only feeds into Singer's anxiety.

Jacob's Ladder creates a great deal of its tension by showing the protagonist's descent into madness. In other films, this story line sometimes comes off as almost laughable, when descending into madness is portrayed with ill-used and cheesy effects and there is little characterization of the protagonist aside from their being mad. The effects here are very convincing and disturbing, used sparingly and quite effectively. The character is worth caring about; he is a three-dimensional human being.

Another of the reasons that *Jacob's Ladder* works is because there are very real motivations for Singer to feel confused and paranoid. He's hallucinating, this is true. Yet, the subway station, where he was nearly killed, was barricaded, preventing him from getting out without risking his life in the tunnels. He is almost run down by a car. His doctor died when his car "exploded." The signs of conspiracy are all around.

This film succeeds in giving the audience a none-too-pleasant taste of what a spiral down into schizophrenia might be like. Singer isn't making up grand stories or having delusions that are obvious inventions of his mind. His world really is becoming more and more bizarre and, because of the way this film carries it all off, it's difficult to tell whether the insanity surrounding the character is actually in Singer's mind or not.

Insanity is as common in thrillers as six-shooters are in westerns. The difference between the insanity theme in *Jacob's Ladder* and that same theme in many other thrillers is easy to illustrate. When Norman Bates starts to exhibit the signs of his insanity, we're afraid *of* him; when Singer starts to show the signs of his insanity, we're afraid *for* him.

The Right Protagonist

Jacob's Ladder also succeeds because the protagonist is a character that most people can instantly feel compassion for. Many men and women return from war damaged to the point that it takes them a lifetime to recover and that is how we initially see Singer. He's a wounded warrior whose battle experiences have apparently shattered his sanity or, at least, have cracked it deeply enough that the pieces start falling away in a truly terrifying sequence of events.

Singer himself is terrified by the hallucinations he's having. His life jolts ahead in fits and starts. In one moment, he's at a party before having a breakdown. The next, he's at his girlfriend's being chastised for his bizarre behavior. The next moment, a group of people are plunging him into a tub full of ice water, trying to bring down a fever, but there's something more sinister than helpful about them.

Farther Down

As Singer's journey continues, the filmmaking style becomes more jarring and disjointed. The flashbacks become more frequent. We see Singer being evacuated via helicopter. Crystal clear shots of palm trees and other jungle scenery clash with gritty, dirty scenes of Singer's life post-war.

Whatever is driving Singer to madness, it becomes apparent to the audience that its roots are in his Vietnam experiences. We're not clear on the real nature of those experiences and, along with the protagonist, we have to start wondering just how shattered they left him. Have all the years since he came home been like this? Did this madness just begin or has it been festering for some time?

We don't know, and Singer doesn't really know, either. It becomes difficult to tell when Singer is awake, asleep or hallucinating.

This journey becomes more painful as the movie plays out. Singer eventually meets up with other people he served with in Vietnam. They tell him that they are having hallucinations as well, and that they feel that they are going insane. The first person to open up to Singer about this, Paul, is killed in a car explosion that nearly kills Singer as well. This is the same way that Singer's doctor was supposed to have died, ratcheting up the conspiracy-driven tension and making it obvious that whatever happened in the opening scenes was somehow at the root of all of this.

The Conspiracy Revealed

Singer's former army buddies meet at Paul's funeral. They've all had bizarre experiences. Other people connected to the happenings have died in mysterious car explosions. Someone's covering something up, as one of them points out. Another just says that "it was bad grass," referencing a joint the soldiers were smoking during the attack that opens up the film.

A conspiracy, no matter how labyrinthine, has to be revealed, if not fully explained, at some point to keep a story interesting. In *Jacob's Ladder*, we find out that the hallucinations are the results of a drug that Jacob's unit was given. The man who reveals the conspiracy is shown helping Singer in the Huey after Singer is injured at the beginning of the film. He claims to have worked for the military under duress on a drug that was given to soldiers. It was designed to make them take a "fast trip straight down the [evolutionary] ladder" into their primal rage. The chemist reveals that the drug was tested on primates and that it made them into utter savages. It was then tested on POWs and it brought out the same horrific violence in them. The army decided to test the drug on Singer's battalion. His battalion responded predictably, and savagely, but they all attacked one another instead of the enemy. Singer's bayonet wound was from one of his comrades, the entire group having gone mad and "torn each other to pieces," as the chemist reveals.

This is a brilliant distraction, it turns out, but also something that does actually play into the reason why Singer's life is taking such a bizarre turn.

Nothing in this film is what it appears to be and, as a masterful thriller is wont to do, this one increases the tension and the confusion just when the audience is led to believe they know what is going on.

It All Comes Clear

There are hints. Jacob asks if he is dead when he wakes up at his girlfriend's house. Time moves in senseless ways. Louie tells Jacob about the theological idea that the flames of hell are there to burn away whatever is holding people back from moving on. He tells Jacob that demons are really angels trying to free the dead from the earth. Louis looks like an angel, as a matter of fact, and, in one of the first post-war scenes in the film, where a chiropractic neck adjustment seems to trigger a flashback, Louis explains that he needed to get deep in there to relieve the pain. A fortuneteller at a party where Singer has a horrific hallucination tells him he has an unusual lifeline. According to what his palm says, Singer is already dead.

When Singer is abducted by a group of men who appear to be government thugs of some type, he fights for his life with uncommon savagery, managing to escape the car into which he has been forced and giving the men who abducted him a vicious beating in the process. He is clearly not ready to die.

The doctors who treat him after he falls out of the car, replying to Singer insisting that he needs to get out of the hospital and just as they're about to perform an utterly terrifying surgery, say, "There is no out of here. You've been killed. Don't you remember?"

We also see Singer lying on his back being treated by various people—girlfriend, neighbors, chiropractor, etc.—mirroring him being treated in the helicopter in Vietnam. Perhaps these are bits of reality slipping into his dying hallucination, reinterpreted so they fit as much as possible within the fantasy life he is living out in his head.

A twist ending cannot be introduced out of the blue, or it just seems cheap and contrived. There has to be some indication that the truth has been apparent, if the story is understood correctly, from the beginning. Without this, the audience will only feel that they have been the victims of lazy writing and lazy plotting.

Jacob Singer was a man who died in Vietnam. The entire movie was played out in his mind. His entire, vast hallucination was only his mind playing out all his regrets, all his fears and anxieties. The demons he saw, as Louis suggested, were only there to free him from the earth and, when he was finally ready to let go, they became angels.

This thriller succeeds on many levels, particularly on levels where other films oftentimes fail. It's terrifying—more so than most horror movies can claim to be—and it's emotionally riveting. The protagonist is believable and relatable. Some viewers will likely have figured out the twist before the end of the movie and others will be surprised to find out the truth. In either case, *Jacob's Ladder* is a fine choice in thrillers for anyone who wants to watch such a film that explores themes dealing with insanity, death, confusion and coming to peace with the darkness in the world and, ultimately, being set free from it.

Singer makes it home at the end. It's not a real home; it's only in his mind. But his son is there waiting for him and, in a not-too-subtle ending, he escorts Jacob up a flight of stairs into a soft, yellow light, just as the chemist back in Vietnam says, "He's gone," and stops administering care. Singer looks peaceful in the end but, as one of the nurses remarks, he put up a hell of a fight, and a thrilling one to watch at that.

Misery: The Contained Thriller (1990)

Director: Rob Reiner

Starring: James Caan

Kathy Bates

Misery is based on the 1987 Steven King novel of the same name. The film was adapted for the screen by William Goldman, writer of other thrillers including *The Marathon Man, Magic* and *The Stepford Wives*. The film is a fine example of a contained thriller and is a fan and critic favorite.

Plot and Setup

Misery comes in at slightly over 90 minutes in length and doesn't waste any time getting to the meat of the story. Paul Sheldon is a famous novelist, a writer of romance stories. He has just completed the latest novel in his series of books featuring a character named Misery Chastain as the film opens. He has a celebratory cigarette and glass of champagne and then takes off in a classic Mustang.

The film, right from the start, pays homage to another famous film based on a King novel, *The Shining*. Sheldon is in the Colorado mountains and the snow is rapidly making the roads impassable. He swerves off of the road, rolls his car and ends up with a pair of broken legs.

He wakes up in the home of Annie Wilkes, who is his "number one fan," as she likes to say. She seems kindly at first. Her excuses for not calling an ambulance or rushing Sheldon to the hospital herself also hold up. The roads are impassable, it's the dead of winter in Colorado so they're not likely to be open anytime soon and, as fortune would have it, Annie is a nurse. She has splinted Sheldon's legs and given him painkillers, putting him up in a cozy bedroom in her home while he convalesces. Everything seems fine at first, even fortunate.

Sheldon soon starts to see that there are some cracks under the surface where Annie's personality is concerned. She quickly angers when she starts talking about the profanity in Sheldon's latest novel. She spills soup on Sheldon at one point, apologizing right away but making it apparent that Sheldon is vulnerable in this situation.

Sheldon's latest *Misery* novel has been released and Annie has picked up the first copy from the local store. She's excited about the book, until she reads far enough to find out that the title character dies.

She flies into a horrifying rage, demonstrating that the woman is clearly insane. She demands that Sheldon write another book in which the title character is resurrected. Paul makes more than one escape attempt during the course of the film, first to get painkillers in an attempt to poison Annie and then to get a knife from the kitchen. Annie's home, unlike Annie herself, is meticulously ordered and she notices a statue out of place, busting Sheldon at trying to escape his room. She references how diamond miners sometimes stole from mines and how an operation called 'hobbling' was used to control them. She then proceeds to break both of Sheldon's ankles in one of the most gut wrenching scenes in the film.

Sheldon hasn't been completely lost to the world. He's considered a missing person and the local sheriff, a man who is obviously very close to retirement, is investigating. The sheriff manages to find some of the same information that Sheldon has found in Annie's house. She was implicated in the murders of infants during her time as a nurse but was never convicted.

He visits Annie, exploring the house and creating some of the tensest moments in the movie in the process. Determining that nothing is amiss, he leaves, but hears Paul calling out for help on his way to the door. He returns and Annie kills him.

Annie has decided that God wanted her to save Sheldon, which means that they both have to die. She has two bullets in her snub-nosed .38, one for each, and approaches Sheldon with a syringe in one hand and the gun in the other.

Sheldon plays into her delusions, saying that they have to finish the book, together, before they both die. Annie agrees.

Sheldon writes out the rest of the book, dumps lighter fluid he sneaked into his room on it and threatens to burn everything when Annie comes into the room. He tosses the match onto the manuscript, Annie dives for it and a great fight scene ensues.

Sheldon survives; Annie doesn't, except in the regard that she haunts him for the rest of his life.

This is one of the best thrillers around that feature themes of confinement and helplessness. It also has some elements in common with other great thrillers.

Paul Sheldon's Ordeal

Paul Sheldon, in many regards, is in a similar situation as Jefferies in *Rear Window*. He's broken his leg in a car accident—legs, in Sheldon's case—is confined to a wheelchair and knows that something very wrong is going on in his surroundings.

His situation differs, however, in that Jefferies gets involved with a murderer of his own volition and from a safe, remote perch. Sheldon is in the murderer's house from the start and he didn't do anything to get there. Jefferies ran out on the track during a car race, receiving an injury that most people would be proud of in the sense that it's something of a battle scar earned in the line of duty. Sheldon got into a random car wreck because of the weather. One man chose his fate through action; one man had no choice in how he ended up.

Sheldon is a very cool customer, given the circumstances. He tries to rationalize with Annie at first but, as he realizes how warped she really is, he starts to figure out how he can either kill her, escape or both. The woman's rages become increasingly intimidating. We constantly see Paul from above, emphasizing his helplessness. After she breaks his ankles, he's in the same situation that Jefferies in *Rear Window* ends up in. The difference is that Jefferies is sleeping peacefully while his beautiful, kind-hearted and very capable girlfriend lazes on the bed nearby, while Sheldon is in a wheelchair, locked into a room with barred windows by a maniac and desperately needs to escape, with his situation getting worse and worse.

Sheldon, however, starts to overcome his sense of helplessness as he recovers. He repeatedly lifts the typewriter to regain the strength in his arms. He starts to realize that, while Annie may be completely maniacal, she is also simple-minded in some regards. She's a religious fanatic who is afraid of profanity, but who is completely comfortable smashing a man's ankles with a hammer. She's disordered, vulnerable in certain ways and certainly subject to being manipulated, but it's more akin to edging one's way through a minefield than it is a simple game of mental domination over someone who's disordered by an intellectually superior and mentally more stable person. Sheldon has power but, to use it, he needs to be patient, clever and on his guard. In the final two acts of this film, it's everything Sheldon can do to avoid being tortured or murdered by the woman.

Sheldon is given plenty of false hope in this film and that's part of what keeps the tension on an ever-increasing curve until the climax. He tries to poison Annie but she spills her wine, spilling the drugs he put in it along with the drink. He tries to hide a knife and her rage over that, in part, is what ends up getting his ankles broken.

Sheldon doesn't give up. He convincingly implies that he wants Annie to be part of the writing process and changes his new novel to fit her critiques. He's only trying to stay alive at this point, but he is starting to get into Annie's head and to gain something of an advantage.

Sheldon, like so many thriller antagonists, could be anyone. Despite his glamorous profession, he's really a very regular guy, at least as he's portrayed. He's not a commando, a former law enforcement officer or a super spy. His legs are broken and, therefore, he's under constant threat. Between how vulnerable he is and how relatable he is, this thriller succeeds in getting the audience to care about the protagonist.

Annie Wilkes

Kathy Bates has a pleasant face and seems about as harmless as anyone could be. Her rendition of Annie in this film is a great demonstration of how fine an actress she is. By the end of the film, she is completely and utterly terrifying. Sure, she wouldn't be a threat to anyone walking down the street, but she doesn't pick her victims like a regular killer might. She believes she has some meaningful connection to her victims, even that God arranged it outside of her own will. She preys on the utterly helpless. The murders for which she was tried involved her killing children while employed as a nurse. Annie Wilkes, in every way, is evil packaged up in a very innocuous, even pleasant wrapping.

But she's cruel. She's cruel beyond belief. When she flies into a rage, her face distorts, she starts spewing a torrent of silly substitutes for profanity and she's willing to torture and even murder as a result of her delusions. She's isolated. Her farm is on a very remote road in the mountains of Colorado. In Sheldon's story, she functions as an ambush predator in every way. The victim not only doesn't see her coming, he thinks she's there to help.

In the scenes where Annie loses her temper, her face fills the screen. These tight shots make the audience feel as if she's raging at them. She becomes full of hate and anger and murder and all of it is petrifying. Even if one didn't have a matching pair of broken legs and was quite capable of taking on Annie physically, it would be frightening. Hers is the face of complete and utter madness.

She uses the skills she's developed—drugs, medical treatments—to torment and confine her victim. She's twisted in this regard, as well; a would-be angel of mercy transformed into an angel of death.

One of the most frightening things about Annie is her sense of self-righteousness. She truly believes that she is a good person and that, in fact, she has divine approval for what she's doing. She is more or less unstoppable in the psychological sense. No matter how much her madness is pointed out to her, she feels she is above any earthly judgment. As is discovered in newspaper articles detailing her trial, she has said so literally, expecting to be judged by a higher power rather than a lowly earthly court.

Whether or not Annie has killed anyone who could have stopped her is never really revealed. Her victims in the hospital were children and the one murder we see on screen is an ambush; she shoots the sheriff in the back. Annie's lethality comes from the strength of her convictions and the fact that, while she may not be all that intelligent, she's cunning.

She's also obsessed. She has a pig named Misery. She knows every detail of Sheldon's life and believes that she is falling in love with him while she is holding him captive.

As far as thriller villains go, it's hard to match Annie Wilkes. She's nearly the definition of the Lawful Evil trope referenced in prior chapters. She believes that she functions in the service of a greater law and that people who somehow deserve to die under that law can be freely killed by her own hand. She is wicked, insane and very motivated. A toxic mix, indeed.

It Just Keeps Getting Worse

This thriller is flawless in how it builds up to its climax. There is very little comic relief. The sheriff and his wife provide some, but most of it just frustrates the audience as there is only so much time before Annie kills Sheldon and the moments that the sheriff and his wife waste on cute banter are running the clock down.

Annie keeps falling apart throughout the film. Her obsession, Sheldon, has disappointed her over and over again and the strain begins to show in her face and her actions. At times, she exhibits the blackest of depressions. In other scenes, she is cheerful and bright, until some random imperfection in Sheldon sets her off again. When Sheldon, with freshly broken ankles, flips her off through the window, she laughs and pretends he's just kidding.

The Tensest Scenes

Some of the tensest scenes in this film rely on subtlety, but there are plenty of scenes that are all-out terrifying as well. When Sheldon, after having made his two escape attempts, wakes to find Annie standing over him with a syringe in her hand, it's definitely a startle moment. Again, she's shown with her face filling the camera, looking every inch the maniac.

When Annie tells the story of hobbling miners to keep them from stealing, the audience is rather certain of what's about to happen and it makes the scene among the most memorable in the film. Watching Sheldon's ankles getting broken is one thing, but it's the lead-up to it that is petrifying. Annie almost mocks the audience, telling Sheldon they're "almost done" after she hammers his first ankle, as if she's a comforting nurse about to finish off an unpleasant procedure.

The third act of this film, and the climax, are the tensest parts of the story, by far. The way they unfold toys with the audience masterfully.

When the sheriff enters Annie's home to look around, he immediately starts turning his back to her. This is enough to set any viewer on edge and, in fact, it seems like something a sheriff with his long years of experience would know better than to do. He wanders through the house but Sheldon is incapacitated in the basement. Over and over again, Annie creeps up behind him. It makes the tension nail-biting in the extreme.

When the sheriff comes back into the house after hearing Sheldon tip over a grill, he stands at the top of the stairs, again with his back to the room, and it proves to be his undoing. As many great thrillers do, this film manages to make the audience even more scared of Annie after she kills him, but also instantly makes the audience feel sad for the murder of the sheriff. We know his wife, they were obviously in love and he was clearly about ready to hang up his sheriff's badge, but all of that is lost because of a maniac who should have been tossed in prison years ago. Such is life in Stephen King's universe, of course.

The Final Confrontation

The final confrontation in this film is perfectly rendered on its own merits. It's also very reminiscent of the final confrontation in *Rear Window*. It is, however, much more brutal than the confrontation in that film.

Sheldon agrees to finish the book so that he and Annie, together, can give Misery eternal life. Annie has already told Sheldon that she has two bullets in her gun.

He works out the manuscript and threatens to burn it, as was said, and then the real terror begins. What ensues is a great portrayal of a real life-or-death struggle between two average people. Neither of these people know how to fight, but both of them are willing to kill.

Sheldon manages to brain Annie with the typewriter, but it doesn't put her out. They roll on the floor, Sheldon getting the upper hand and stuffing her mouth with the burning manuscript. He sticks his thumbs in her eyes and thinks that he's killed her but, of course, any viewer is going to be screaming for him to hit her again, just to be sure, as he crawls away.

Of course, she's not dead. She manages to get up and attack Sheldon again and they both struggle on the floor. He picks up a sculpture of a pig that's fallen to the floor and smashes it into her head, finally killing her.

Between beating the woman with a typewriter and hitting her with a sculpture of a pig—her pet pig is named Misery—the symbolism here is really not all that subtle. Somehow, however, and in a very dark sense, it provides a bit of comic relief in the middle of an incredibly frightening fight scene.

Here's where one can really start to see some comparisons to *Rear Window*.

In many scenes, Wilkes is filmed in a very similar fashion to how Hitchcock filmed Thorwald, the murderer in *Rear Window*. They both dominate the screen and their eyes are murderous. Like Jefferies, Sheldon has to struggle for his life in a wheelchair and ends up using the instrument with which he both makes his living and which, at a certain level, is responsible for him getting his legs broken as a way to defend himself, and cleverly so. Jefferies used the flash on his camera to blind Thorwald; Sheldon uses a typewriter to bludgeon Annie. Likewise, Jefferies's camera and Sheldon's typewriter are both what got them into their awful messes in the first place.

Both films play into themes of alienation. The protagonist in both films is isolated from the world, one surrounded by good people and one imprisoned by a lunatic, but isolated nonetheless. Their isolation, in both cases, plays into their vulnerability.

This film also invokes *The Shining* rather strongly. Each film relies on isolating its protagonist in a Colorado winter to set up the plot. Each one involves a writer who is dealing with madness, either their own or someone else's. Both films also use the fact that it's nearly impossible for help to find them to ratchet the tension up and both have murderous conclusions. There is nothing supernatural about *Misery* and, of course, the Overlook Hotel in *The Shining* is haunted, making them a thriller and a horror film, respectively, but they do share some interesting similarities.

Why This Film Works

As far as modern thrillers go, *Misery* is among the best of the best. King and Goldman are both excellent writers who know how to scare an audience. Both of them, in fact, have used seemingly mild-mannered characters who are, in truth, as barking mad as antagonists in their other tales. This, of course, is nothing new, but Goldman and King both do it remarkably well.

Misery is contained in more ways than one. One could even call it a confined thriller, because that theme constitutes the origin of much of its tension.

When Annie's madness comes forth, her face is barely contained by the edges of the screen. When she's not having an episode, she's so sickly sweet that it's almost as menacing as her madness.

The film, because it has so few characters and settings, also succeeds in drawing the audience into the personalities involved—however disordered they may be—and that makes it compelling to watch. We want to see Sheldon survive, somehow, but it's sure hard not to want to see just how mad Annie really is. She doesn't disappoint in this regard.

This is a great thriller for the intellectual who wants to see madness up close and personal. It's also a great thrill for the person who prefers more visceral thrills, as it has plenty of them. It's tight, compact and Reiner does a great job of making the look and feel of the film suit the story. For thrillers employing themes of victimization, isolation, madness and the urge to escape, it would be hard to do better than *Misery*.

Pay particularly close attention to Bates' performance in this film. Annie's insanity, in the hands of a lesser actress, could well have come off as comical, even cheesy. In Bates' capable hands, however, it's unforgettable. Bates gets a lot of praise for her work in this role and both she and Caan deserve it. It's a well-written, well-made and well-executed film in every regard.

The Silence of the Lambs (1991): Killers, Madness and Beyond

Director: Jonathan Demme

Starring: Jodie Foster

Anthony Hopkins

The Silence of the Lambs is not an easily forgotten film. Based on a 1988 novel by Thomas Harris, it launched several sequels and was preceded by a film that took place in the same universe, *Manhunter*, which did not get the same high praise as a film as does *The Silence of the Lambs*.

The Silence of the Lambs is a classic thriller that will appeal to anyone who loves crime thrillers, a dash of noir and a lot of terror. This film succeeds on many different levels and Anthony Hopkins and Jodie Foster do a particularly effective job of bringing the pure evil of the Hannibal Lecter character to life through their dialogues in the film.

This film is considered so good, in fact, that it was entered into the U.S. Library of Congress National Film Registry as of 2011.

The Plot

Part of the reason that *The Silence of the Lambs* succeeds is because of the complexity of the plot. There is actually more than one plot in this film. The first involves a manhunt by the FBI for a serial killer they have come to call Buffalo Bill. The second involves Hannibal Lecter and his relationship with Clarice Starling, an FBI agent who interviews him to get information about the serial killer that the FBI believes may help them find Buffalo Bill.

Lecter is not only a serial killer himself—a cannibal, no less—but is also an accomplished psychiatrist. Given his predilection for murder and cannibalism, he most certainly understands the dark side of the human psyche. Buffalo Bill is certainly firmly on that side of the psyche.

Buffalo Bill's MO is to kidnap and kill women. Following their murders, he skins the women and sticks a particularly rare type of moth down their throats. The countdown clock in this movie is set up via the abduction of a senator's daughter. The senator has the power to kick the investigation into high gear, she does, and Starling is given the job of interviewing Lecter about the murders, as his combination of being a brilliant psychiatrist and a serial killer makes him uniquely qualified to understand the motivations and methods of serial killers.

Lecter is smart enough to know when he has leverage and uses it to try to get transferred to a new facility, given the director of the one he's currently at torments him. He also wants to get into Clarice Starling's head and he does, quite well.

Lecter eventually manages to make his way to Tennessee, being taken there as part of the investigation into finding the senator's daughter. While there, he manages to get Starling to tell him a story, from which the name of the movie and book are taken. Clarice witnessed the slaughter of lambs at a farmhouse and sometimes can still hear the lambs screaming as they were killed. This story actually ends up forging something of a bond between Lecter and Starling, which is explored later on in the series.

Lecter manages to escape custody in a truly gut-wrenching sequence.

Starling manages to track down Buffalo Bill using good detective skills. She finds his lair and, in one of the tensest scenes in the film, is pursued by Buffalo Bill through his basement, a scene we see through Bill's night-vision goggles.

Lecter, at the end of the film, is shown calling Starling from the Bahamas, where he is already following Chilton, the director of the institution where he was imprisoned and Lecter's former tormentor. Lecter plans to kill and eat the man.

Delving into the Darkness

Silence of the Lambs, when broken down to a summary, sounds much less powerful than the film actually is. What makes this film so memorable is how dark it is. The killers in this film are sadistic, creative and very good at what they do. Buffalo Bill doesn't have Lecter's refinement or intelligence, but he's cunning and determined and, on top of it, utterly insane. Lecter is a wildcard. He's so intelligent and reserved—most of the time—that it's easy to forget how awful he truly is. Hopkins' portrayal makes the viewer want to like Lecter. He's charming, but as Gavin De Becker, author of *The Gift of Fear,* said, "Charm is a verb."

Lecter is very, very charming. When he adds to his list of demands for helping the investigation that Clarice start telling him about her past, it almost seems like he wants to help. He wants to know what darkness she has inside of her and, in fact, what better guide through that darkness could one have than Hannibal Lecter? It's tempting; appropriately so, given that Lecter is so wicked and capable that he nearly comes off as the devil himself. The man knows what makes humans weak; that much is certain.

Clarice tries to play the game herself. The offer of a transfer to a different prison that she presents Lecter is a ruse. The FBI believes that it has something that makes Lecter weak. Unfortunately, whether it's plot convenience or not, things tend to go Lecter's way in this film. Chilton, the prison administrator, finds out that the deal isn't real and tells Lecter. He offers Lecter a deal of his own. Making a deal with him goes about as well as one would expect. Lecter's always a few steps ahead.

He gets everything he wanted out of the deal after he gets to Tennessee. He gets information about Clarice's past out of her, her most painful memory, in fact. He then gets his freedom, and in the most gruesome way possible. He kills two guards and fakes his own death. As the ambulance drives who they believe to be an injured guard away from the scene of the escape, Lecter is actually revealed to have disguised himself by using a dead guard's face as a mask.

How Is He Possibly Charming?

Given what Lecter does in the film, it's hard to imagine how anyone could consider this man charming, or even potentially so. One of the things that makes this thriller work so well is that the dialogue between Starling and Lecter seems genuine and, to some extent, it seems like he's actually growing to enjoy Starling. One of the sources of very dark comic relief in the Lecter character is that he cannot tolerate rude people and he has a particular way of dealing with people he cannot tolerate, of course. Starling is intelligent, quick, a good conversationalist and she doesn't condescend to Lecter. She's polite and intelligent and Lecter—as much as he can be said to feel so of anyone—seems to like her.

This fits in with the overall backstory for Lecter. Lecter was, because of his genuine skill and knowledge in the field of psychology and his financial wherewithal, part of very polite society. He surrounded himself with the finer things in life and with people who were charming, witty and intelligent. Perhaps he sees some of this in Starling, even though he busts her hiding her rural roots. Starling is genuinely more than the sum of her parts and she's good at what she does. Lecter seems to appreciate that. Given how he dealt with a flautist who fell short during a performance, it's good to be thought of highly by this character.

There is another layer to this. Lecter seems to know full well that he's evil. He really is, in many regards, guiding Starling through a world that, as a soon-to-be special agent, she really only dabbles in. Lecter understands human darkness from the level of someone who has not only studied and analyzed it to great success and in depth, but also as someone who embodies it.

Lecter is, in some ways, the opposite of Starling. He comes from refined roots but his real nature landed him in the bottommost level of a maximum-security prison. Clarice comes from the lower economic class, but her real nature has landed her at the highest levels of law enforcement. They're both brilliant, but their trajectories are exactly the opposite relative to where they started out in life, simply because of the kind of people they are at the core of them.

Buffalo Bill

Buffalo Bill is nearly as memorable as Lecter, but not for his intelligence or charm. This man is completely insane and bizarre. His grand plan is to construct a suit made of the skin of dead women so that he himself can become a woman, at least in his own mind. He has skills as a dressmaker and is well into the process of constructing his suit, the senator's daughter having been chosen as another source of fabric, as it were. The fact that he targets larger women provides one of the clues to what he's doing to the investigators.

Buffalo Bill is, to some degree, modeled on Ed Gein, a serial killer operating in Wisconsin during the 1950s. He became notorious for having various shrunken heads, parts of bodies and human skins that he had crafted into an array of clothing and other items at his home when he was discovered. Like Buffalo Bill, Gein wanted to use the skin of dead women to make a woman suit for himself. This is very much paralleled in *The Silence of the Lambs*. One of the more frightening implications of this film is that, while Hannibal Lecter is said, in his backstory as related in other stories in this series, to match no psychological profile recorded, Buffalo Bill most certainly does. There was a Buffalo Bill in real life and, as far as his murderous nature goes, he's no less terrifying than Lecter, save for the fact that his MO is drawn from real life.

Buffalo Bill's real name is Jame Gumb. Gumb is revealed to have a history of mental illness and murder as a child. He acquired his tailoring skills while he was being held in an asylum and, upon going back to the outside world, murdered one of his lovers.

Transgenderism and Serial Killers in Thrillers

Aside from the Ed Gein parallel, there is obviously some parallel characterization between Buffalo Bill and Normal Bates of *Psycho*. In both of these films, it has been argued, the transgender activities of characters like Gumb and Bates are used as ways to make them monstrous in the eyes of the audience. This is likely true, to some degree, and strong arguments are made for it.

In *The Silence of the Lambs*, however, there is a different way to look at the situation that can make the film seem even more layered. When the ugliest side of Gumb comes out, it's very male: "Put the f&%king lotion in the basket!" His feminine side comes out and is quite apologetic afterward, which is noted in the link above.

This is interesting, in that the transgendered side of Gumb is assumed to be gentler and more humane than his masculine side. In reality, however, the novels do away with these arguments handily. Gumb is not actually transgendered at all. He hates himself and being male is part of his identity and, therefore, he wants to change it. While Gumb may have convinced himself that he's transgendered, an informed audience knows better. Gumb's insanity has to do with his detachment from his identity as a whole, his murderous rages and his delusions.

Gumb, like many serial killers, feels motivated to leave a calling card. He leaves a death's-head hawkmoth in the throats of his victims. Starling later sees the moth in the house to which she's tracked him, confirming that she's found the killer.

There is the whole symbolism argument to be made about Gumb transforming himself, as a moth does when it changes from a caterpillar to a full-fledged moth. In reality, Gumb is everything he'll ever be at the start of this movie. He's insane, murderous and utterly driven by his own delusions.

One could interpret this film, the story and the characters endlessly. Roger Ebert, famously no fan of films that wasted his time, participated in a frame-by-frame analysis of the film himself and found much depth. The killers in this film provide some of the richest ground for interpretation of all and, to a great degree, that's what makes this film so involving.

Clarice Gets Her Killer

The climax of *The Silence of the Lambs* is probably one of the most intense sequences ever put to film. It takes place in the basement of the house that Starling has tracked Gumb to, in the dark basement where he's constructing his macabre suit.

We see the most intense parts of the sequence through Gumb's eyes. He's wearing night-vision goggles that he put on before killing the lights. Starling gropes around in the dark, terrified, and utterly helpless as Gumb stalks her through the rooms. Her heavy breathing betrays her terror; her eyes huge, looking for any way to orient herself in the dark and for the man who's obviously lurking within it.

At the end of the film, we also get to see a little, perhaps, of what Lecter admired in Starling. Gumb cocks his pistol and, rather than freezing, Starling opens fire toward the sound. The flashes of gunfire illuminate the darkness, allowing Starling to acquire her target. It's not clear whether Gumb misses because he's already been shot or if he just doesn't have Starling's training and collected nature to rely upon, but he falls to the ground, dying, and the scene is lit as one of Starling's stray shots puts out a blacked-out basement window.

Starling not only doesn't freeze, she reloads her gun and is ready for Gumb to get up again, though she's already mortally wounded him. In the end, we see that Starling is not a naïve FBI agent being toyed with by far more dangerous foes. Because of her intelligence, her ability to hold it together under stress and her will to survive, she's quite capable and, ultimately, proves to be the end of Jame Gumb.

Why This Film Works

The Silence of the Lambs is widely regarded as one of the best films of its kind. In fact, it's so good that, in some ways, it's genre-defying. It's every bit as frightening as most horror films, but more so, in many ways. It's an incredible, pure thriller in that the entire film depends on constant tension. Somehow, this film manages to keep the audience on the edge of their seats—and likely hiding under a blanket at times—through its entire runtime. It does this without wearing the audience out. None of the plot points turn out to be dead ends, and the audience is never insulted by being made to feel silly about giving the film their full attention.

The film, in many ways, is a lot like Lecter himself. It's highbrow, but also deals with the basest instincts and most brutal parts of the human psyche. It tells its story in clear, refined tones, but the story is ultimately one that is grotesque in the extreme. It gives the audience a killer drawn from real life, demonstrating that the disturbing nature of the events depicted in the film is not pure fantasy, but gives the audience an incredibly memorable fantasy serial killer in Hannibal Lecter himself.

The protagonist of the film isn't the best agent in the FBI and, in fact, isn't even a full Special Agent until the very end of the film. She is, however, well ahead of the other people working on the case in how she puts everything together. She's not the strongest or most intimidating specimen of a federal agent, to be sure, but she's well-trained, committed and certainly up to the task of defending herself when the situation calls for it, achieving deadly results against a seasoned, psychopathic killer when she's at an unimaginable disadvantage.

The impressive thing about *The Silence of the Lambs* is that the audience appreciates these twists and turns. They never come off as cheap or contrived. This is a film for grownups, to be sure, and it's one that's not particularly innovative in its most basic sense. It's about law enforcement agents trying to profile, identify and find a serial killer before he kills the damsel in distress, which is certainly nothing new. The way it offers up this very standard scenario, however, is done with such a degree of excellence that the audience doesn't mind or even realize that they're being told a classic story of good pursuing evil with some new ingredients added in to make it more interesting. In the end, it's done very well and, perhaps, is the type of gourmet cinematic fare that would go well with some fava beans and a nice Chianti.

http://3riversdefense.com/?p=316

http://www.wisconsinsickness.com/ed-gein/

http://keyboardsmash.wordpress.com/category/trans-canon/

http://books.google.com/books?id=SQqqX1EIG2gC&pg=PA137&lpg=PA137&dq=silence+of+the+lambs+moth+metaphor&source=bl&ots=K8EO92pBev&sig=9vBPieRxVUgcGd3c3Fka289mhbs&hl=en&sa=X&ei=H7p6UrS6IuSEjALT_4DYCg&ved=0CDcQ6AEwAg#v=onepage&q=silence%20of%20the%20lambs%20moth%20metaphor&f=false

http://www.rogerebert.com/rogers-journal/22-secrets-gleaned-from-silence

Se7en: Dark, Grimy and Terrifying (1995)
Director: David Fincher

Starring: Brad Pitt

Morgan Freeman

Gwyneth Paltrow

Kevin Spacey

Se7en is a film that rattles a lot of people's cages. It's one of the darkest films around, for certain, and the eerie sort of 'any city at any time' atmosphere it creates is really, truly unpleasant. This is the kind of film that makes everything in your house feel dirty after you watch it. It takes the worst elements of decay—urban, psychological, moral and beyond—and combines them into a horrid storm of awfulness that makes the viewer at once glad they do not live in this fictional city where it always rains, but quite aware that the killer in this film could be their neighbor, for there is nothing remarkable about him save for his utter savagery and deranged conviction that he is a paragon of morality.

Se7en is, in many regards, one of the best thrillers out there and quite possibly among the top two or three of the 1990s.

The Setting and Setup
Se7en shows off one of the elements of good storytelling right from the start. The entire plot can be broken down into a very short—one sentence, actually—synopsis that is compelling in and of itself. Two police officers have to track down a brutal serial killer before he kills again.

This isn't an original plot, of course, particularly among thriller movies, but it is always a good one to go with if you want to keep people's attention on the screen. What this film does very well and, in fact, what makes *Se7en* stand out from many other thriller films, is that there is always an element underpinning every scene that makes the viewer wonder if it's really even worth it to stop this particular serial killer. The city in which *Se7en* takes place is never named, but it could be the worst part of most any large city out there. Just about every living space is dingy and unpleasant; some of them are outright revolting. It is usually raining in this city. Because of that, not only is everything dingy and dirty, but there is the implication that the atmosphere must be humid, rancid and just as dirty as the look of the film.

It's Always Raining

Se7en takes a very big risk in the fact that, in the city in which it is set, it is almost always raining. In fact, this is played up to such an extent that if the film hadn't been carried off so masterfully, it would've almost been comical. The city where Somerset and Mills work looks like one that nobody should even waste their time trying to keep safe. It looks like a place where nobody in his or her right mind would ever want to live.

The sets and the technology in the film are featured in ways that make it possible that *Se7en* could happen in just about any era. Nothing about the sets or the props that the characters use makes the film seem dated, even 10 years after it was released.

Se7en does exactly what a good thriller film should do. It sets up a very distinctive world in which the characters play out the drama. It doesn't, however, make that world so distinctive that it becomes distracting to the story. In a sense, the setting of the movie does function somewhat like a character. It is moody, dark, dirty and extremely hard.

Nothing about the universe in which *Se7en* takes place is designed to make the viewer want to hang around for very long. This isn't a setting where anybody watching the film would even be particularly happy to drive through, much less stop and walk around. This is ideal for a thriller film, as all of this is entirely possible. There is nothing fantastic, futuristic or dated about the way *Se7en* looks and feels. This leaves it to the characters to pull the viewers in and, in fact, this movie does an excellent job of providing characters capable of doing so.

Twisting the Protagonist

Se7en, being a thriller film, has ample license to engage in plot twists and in setups that are only revealed to the audience to have been taking place across the entirety of the film in its very last moments. This film excels in using these tools to draw the audience in and to make the entire story even more horrific.

Many thriller films do depend, to some extent, on showing how the events of the film end up changing the protagonists. The characters in *Se7en* encounter something horrible and are forever changed by it.

In *Se7en*, there really isn't any upside to the way the film unfolds. It is never sunny, in other words. If you plan on sitting down and watching *Se7en*, do not anticipate that you are going to get your regular Hollywood fare. This film takes risks. *Se7en* takes the viewer to a very unpleasant place, and, in that regard, it delivers as a thriller film.

The Story

As was stated in the intro, the plot of *Se7en*, in the broadest terms, is really quite simple. It is, in fact, a classic detective story, but a very dark one. In many regards, it isn't that much different than *M* in the basics of its plot. While this murderer may not be a child murderer, he is every bit as horrific and there is just as much impetus for the detectives to track him down, catch him and stop him from committing any further murders.

Starting with the detectives, Detective Somerset and Detective Mills really can be understood to represent two thriller movie archetypes. Detective Somerset is close to retirement, obviously very tired of his job but, at the same time, he is supremely competent at it. He understands how the city he works in operates, he understands what makes for good police work and he is an exceptionally literate man. All of these things will ultimately serve to guide his younger partner, Detective Mills, and will provide the most progress in tracking down the killer.

Detective Mills is married, only recently transferred to the department and, although he's not aware of it, is about to become a father. Mills is far more idealistic and energetic than Detective Somerset, but he lacks the skill and experience that Somerset exhibits. His journey through the film is a compelling one. Mills makes genuine progress in becoming a very good detective. He also does very well at lending what he has to offer to the partnership he has with Somerset, chasing down the killer through an apartment building at one point, for example, which is likely something that Somerset would've had much less success doing, given his being close to retirement age.

Mills is emotional, somewhat egotistical, but, ultimately, at the root of it, he is a good person. The audience doesn't feel uncomfortable identifying with Mills and, in fact, Brad Pitt pulls off the character in a way that, when he is at his most youthful, idealistic and hardheaded, he is also still quite endearing. Somerset is portrayed by Morgan Freeman as a truly wise and steady character. One of the interesting things about this character is that the audience does get the impression that he is someone who has probably seen things worse than most people can imagine, but who retains a very pragmatic and morally trustworthy core. Detective Somerset may not be as fleet of foot as his younger partner, but he is absolutely somebody who one can depend on without feeling like they are putting too much faith into somebody who will not live up to it.

The result is that the viewer genuinely likes the characters in this movie. They are all sympathetic in their own ways and they all have flaws that make them human. While the two detectives may be, in many regards, conventional as thriller protagonists, they are also unique enough to be memorable and, more importantly, they come across as real human beings to the extent that it is quite possible for the audience to worry about them.

What makes *Se7en* so engaging and so memorable as a film is that this film ends up in such a dark place that the audience doesn't feel like they were tricked into worrying about the characters for no good reason. If you haven't seen this film, don't kid yourself: these characters are in very real danger and that danger is, arguably, one that presents a threat even worse than losing one's life.

The Killer

The killer in this movie is simply known as John Doe. There's nothing remarkable about John Doe as a person. He's played by Kevin Spacey. Spacey, when he finally is revealed to be the killer, excepting some very purposeful injuries that he inflicted upon himself, looks so bland that the effect is terrifying. After the murders that this man has committed have been revealed to the audience, the audience is set up to expect a monster. At the very least, they are set up to expect somebody who must be physically terrifying. Kevin Spacey's character is neither. He's so normal that it makes it all the more chilling to think about how easily he could be any person on any street in any city at any time.

John Doe is a religiously and morally motivated serial killer. His murders serve to make examples of his victims by having them atone for one of the seven deadly sins that he has decided they embody. The punishments that he takes out on his victims are ironic. That would be enough of a setup for a film to make for some very disturbing scenes. *Se7en* takes this much, much further. Not only are the murders that John Doe sets up designed to punish the victim in some ironic fashion for the sin he believes that they have committed, they are designed to be as torturous as possible. They are psychologically and physically examples of some of the most brutal and, at the same time, creative sadism imaginable.

The killer in this film works on several different levels. First, he has a mentality that the movie isn't required to make up psychology to explain. There is nothing about the character that requires the audience to swallow some sort of hokey pseudoscience about human behavior for them to understand what is motivating this killer.

In many films, the convention has been to go for fictional versions or pop culture versions of psychology to explain a killer. This has been attempted in horror films, notably the Rob Zombie reboot of the original *Halloween* movie. *Se7en* does delve into the psychology of the killer, but the psychology that emerges is much more terrifying than explaining away the killer as simply being an abused child who grew up into an abusive of adult or, as in some films, an outright murderous adult.

John Doe is motivated to commit his crimes because he sincerely believes that his victims embody one of the seven deadly sins to such an extent that they deserve to die. He is the crusader type of a killer. He not only believes but explicitly states at one point in the movie that he is functioning to clean up society from the types of people who are dragging it down wholesale.

The movie manages to offer this type of a character to the audience without once making the audience feel sympathetic to that character, which is no small feat. Many movies take the opposite tack.

For instance, the *Dirty Harry* franchise centers on a police detective who routinely murders bad people and who the audience sympathizes with because he is cleaning up the streets. Likewise, the *007* franchise has as its protagonist a ruthless assassin and spy who is arguably exactly the same as the people he kills, the only substantial difference being that James Bond happens to be on the right side. In *Se7en* the audience will not for a moment feel like they are being asked to sympathize with somebody who breaks the law to punish the miscreants in society. John Doe is a character with whom it is utterly impossible for any normal human being to sympathize. He is cruel, judgmental, obviously psychopathic, probably psychotic, and sees himself as the enforcer of God's will on Earth. This makes him a remarkably frightening character.

What's worse: John Doe is entirely willing to die for his imaginary cause.

The Setup

The film quickly moves to the first murder. A man has been forced to feed himself to death, embodying the sin of gluttony. *Se7en* not only wastes no time in getting to the meat of the story, it immediately shoves the viewer's face into an enormously repulsive setting. The poor victim's house is difficult to look at, such is the level of filth.

The killer continues on his spree, killing a lawyer for the sin of greed and killing another victim for the sin of sloth. Each of these murders plays out in a way appropriate—from John Doe's twisted perspective—to the sin that the person has been judged as committing. The lawyer is forced to give up a pound of his flesh. The man who was the victim of John Doe for the sin of sloth actually lives. The fact that he is alive provides one of the film's best and most effective startle moments. When the detectives track down this particular victim, they find him strapped to a bed, where he has been kept for a year.

A subplot in the film involves Detective Mills and his wife, Tracy, played by Gwyneth Paltrow. Tracy is pregnant and, after giving the matter some serious consideration, has decided to keep her child. Detective Mills is not yet aware that she is pregnant, but she does confide this to detective Somerset.

Some of the moments that really make the audience care about the characters happen in the interactions between the two detectives and Tracy. For example, at a dinner party scene, Detective Somerset makes a joke about the vibrations from the trains that pass by Detective Mills' apartment that is genuinely funny, delivered perfectly and that creates one of the most endearing moments in the entire film. It contrasts the humanity of the characters with the inhumanity of the environment in which they live. The end result, really, is that it gives the audience even more of an emotional investment in the characters, given that the dinner scene is full of moments that are so common and so universal that it's easy to believe that these are real people.

The Procedural Element

One of the ways in which the story unfolds in *Se7en* is interesting to contrast with the film *M*. In *Se7en*, a great deal of emphasis is put on the really quite brilliant police work that Morgan Freeman's character engages in to catch John Doe. Freeman's character is established as being a literate man at the beginning of the story. It is this literacy and understanding of theology that allows Detective Somerset to begin to understand the motivations and predict the actions of John Doe.

This is an interesting contrast to *M*. *M*, even though it portrays the police force as ultimately failing society due to its inability to track down the murderer, does show the police using very scientific and methodical techniques to do their best to track down the killer. In *Se7en*, Detective Somerset is obviously a methodical and logical man, but it is knowledge of classic literature and a willingness to go to a library and dig through books that really give him the information that he needs.

Most thrillers that involve a crime-and-punishment element—or a cops and robbers element—do show the police procedures to some extent. It is a very effective and very enjoyable way to unfold the plot for the audience and it allows them to participate to some degree, seeing if they can guess what the police will find out next.

In *Se7en*, this procedural element not only serves the aforementioned ends, but it allows the filmmakers to take the film to an entirely other level of darkness. Once it becomes apparent how this killer is operating, it also becomes apparent to the audience that whatever he does next is likely to be just as horrific or even more horrific than what he has already done.

The Thrillers

To get some of its most effective scares, all *Se7en* has to do is show us some of the evidence. For example, it shows us a sex toy device—or a horrible variation on one—that is used to murder a prostitute and, without ever showing the actual murder taking place graphically, it manages to turn any sane person's stomach over at least once.

A victim who John Doe believes has committed the sin of pride is psychologically tortured in the most effective way imaginable for such a person, to the extent that she takes her own life. Everybody who John Doe manages to kill dies a horrible death. The procedural element of the story reveals all of this in a most gut-wrenching way. We see it, for the most part, through the eyes of the detectives and, because of the very effective portrayals by Pitt and Freeman, we are allowed to share in their revulsion.

Telltale Signs of Psychosis/Psychopathy

John Doe, when his apartment is discovered, is revealed to exhibit many of the signs that thriller movies oftentimes rely upon to connote that a character is truly insane. His apartment is filled with notebooks that are packed with his own writings, all of which appear in tiny script, allowing him to stuff even more into each notebook.

His writings are largely about his disdain for society at large, showing his penchant for passing judgment, his obsessive nature and other examples of him being clearly not sane.

John Doe actually turns himself in. In another dark twist, the police prove ultimately unable to capture the man and have to wait for him to surrender himself before they can be sure that the murders are going to stop.

When John Doe does turn himself in, yet another example of exactly how far this man is willing to go is revealed. He has actually cut off his fingerprints to prevent himself from being identified. Once the audience sees this, it is apparent that they are, even though he may look perfectly normal, dealing with an absolute monster.

Not a Happy Ending

It's not unacceptable for a thriller to have a happy ending. Even some of Alfred Hitchcock's thriller movies have what amount to happy endings. Things are resolved; good people, at least to some degree, get rewarded for being good and so forth.

None of that happens in *Se7en*.

John Doe offers to take the detectives out to the scene of the two crimes that they have not been able to find on their own. He makes a legal threat that is a fairly common trope in thriller movies, but that doesn't actually hold up in real life. John Doe offers to admit to his crimes, provided the detectives let him take them out to recover the bodies of his other two victims, or he will plead insanity, presumably avoiding any punishment.

While this setup does work very well for thriller films, it doesn't really pan out in reality. John Doe probably would have been looking at a life sentence in prison, at best, and most likely execution. Going to an asylum for the criminally insane would mean sitting out a life sentence as well. Any thriller film does rely upon the audience accepting some things that don't exactly make sense. In fact, this is sometimes called <u>refrigerator logic</u>. The idea is that, after you watch something happen in a movie or a television show, you don't realize that it didn't make any sense until you go to the refrigerator sometime after.

Why the detectives have to go out to the middle of the desert—and why a major city where it is apparently always raining and a desert are located so close to one another—is really not apparent. After all, what would be the difference between John Doe spending his life in an asylum for the criminally insane and spending his life in a prison? Either way, he's gone forever and, even if he uses the asylum to avoid execution, what's the difference, other than he disappears because he's dead or he disappears because he's never getting out?

Of course, the detectives take the deal and drive out to the desert. On the way out there, a bit of foreshadowing is given to the audience. John Doe toys with Detective Mills. As the expression goes, he starts talking to Detective Mills and 'gets in his head'.

Detective Somerset, on the other hand, uses the time to try to figure out more about John Doe. Where Detective Mills is embodying the moral outrage that the audience would feel toward the killer, who is, perhaps ironically, himself motivated by moral outrage, Detective Somerset embodies the curiosity of the audience.

As is the case with so many different things in this movie, it won't really matter in the end. Nothing turns out well.

Two more victims need to be accounted for. There are two more sins that need to be punished: envy and wrath.

A deliveryman starts coming down the road where Detective Somerset, Detective Mills and John Doe are all being watched over by a helicopter carrying a sniper. Detective Somerset stops the deliveryman and retrieves a box that was supposed to be delivered at the time that the trio is out at the location.

This setup works because it has already been established that John Doe is a murderer who is not averse to engaging in long-term planning. He had kept his sloth victim captive for a full year, indicating that he did plan this out to an obsessive degree of detail. What is about to happen will demonstrate just how cold, calculating and brutally efficient this killer is.

Detective Somerset begins to open the box. "It's blood," he says as he opens the flaps. At the same time, John Doe begins explaining to Detective Mills how much John Doe envies him. Envy. Somerset opens the box, he's terrified, he tells the helicopter to stay away and that "John Doe has the upper hand."

The next three or four minutes unfold with unrelenting tension. John Doe starts explaining to Detective Mills how he broke into Mills' house and tried to "play husband" with Tracy Mills. It didn't work out, he says coldly, and he took a souvenir.

Tracy's head is in the box. Detective Somerset pleads with Detective Mills not to shoot John Doe. He yells to Mills to throw his gun down as he runs up and stands between the two, holding out his arms, trying to explain to Detective Mills that John Doe will win if Mills shoots him.

John Doe eggs Detective Mills on, begging him to become the embodiment of wrath, of vengeance. John Doe gets his wish. Detective Mills, after Brad Pitt gives what has to be one of the best performances of a person literally losing their mind on the spot, shoots John Doe in the head, walks up to the body and shoots him several more times. Detective Somerset looks on, and looks more saddened by what has happened than mortified.

This movie doesn't end in a good place. Everyone John Doe comes into contact with is forever changed for the worse. Detective Mills is a sympathetic character and, in fact, his wife is even more so. Detective Somerset is a character that doesn't deserve to live in the brutal world he lives in, but who is also uniquely equipped to survive it.

This isn't a thriller that will leave you with the pleasant rush you might get after you ride a roller coaster. You will, if this thriller works for you, really feel quite awful after having watched it.

Se7en does deserve the credit it gets for being a great thriller movie. Brad Pitt, Morgan Freeman, Gwyneth Paltrow and Kevin Spacey are all excellent in this movie. This movie is definitely one to watch if you want to experience a thriller film that will take you to places dark enough that they will leave an impression on you to the extent that you well very may, to some degree, judge films you see based upon how they stack up against this one in terms of setting. It's also a great film to watch if you want to experience a story that shows a killer with no redeeming qualities, no sympathetic elements and, in fact, nothing to offer other than pure terror.

Se7en is a fine film, and one that fans of the gritty 1990s movie aesthetic and the darkest kinds of thriller films will likely very much enjoy.

http://tvtropes.org/pmwiki/pmwiki.php/Main/FridgeLogic

Memento (2000): The Cycle of Madness

Director: Christopher Nolan

Starring: Guy Pearce

Carrie-Anne Moss

Joe Pantoliano

Memento is a perplexing film, and that's the point. This 2000 psychological thriller takes the audience on a trip that is sometimes so multi-layered and intricate that it's often difficult to follow the story. This is sometimes the mark of a great thriller and, in fact, it is in this particular case.

Memento is not a film that you can casually watch, getting up every now and then to raid the fridge or just wander off. You have to pay attention to every second of it to understand what's going on. The reward is well worth it. This is a tight thriller that's deceptively wrapped up in a very complex package. Once the ending reveal comes around, you'll likely want to watch it again and will most certainly appreciate what a long, strange trip this film has been.

The Plot and Setup

Memento doesn't move in the linear fashion that most stories use. It unfolds backwards, in fact, and the beginning of the film won't make complete sense to the audience until they make it to the end. This is part of what makes *Memento* so gripping. There is a pervasive sense of disorientation to the entire film that makes it hard to follow at times, and that's precisely the point.

Leonard Shelby (Pearce) is the protagonist of the film. He suffers from anterograde amnesia. This condition is a bit different than the type of amnesia that most audiences will have seen used as a plot device. Rather than not being able to remember his past, Leonard cannot remember anything new. His brain, as the result of an attack in which his wife was murdered, cannot form new memories. This is an actual illness that can, in fact, be brought about by brain trauma, among other causes.

This sets up a constant timer for the audience, in that Leonard only has literally minutes to write down anything that happens to him before it simply fades into oblivion forever. One of the reasons that this film works is the fact that there is never a break from this particular countdown. It also works in setting up Leonard as a sympathetic protagonist, in that, throughout the film, the audience is treated to incidents where his condition is exploited by people for various reasons. It's impossible to tell whether or not Leonard is actually working on good information or if he is being deceived by the people who have figured out how to manipulate him due to his lack of an ability to form new memories. The audience participates fully in the protagonist's confusion and this makes us feel for him.

The condition is portrayed accurately in the film in that Leonard clearly remembers all of the events leading up to his injury, including his former life. As the story progresses, however, it will become clear that even Leonard has figured out ways to manipulate himself, using his condition as a way to give his life purpose. In fact, a great deal of this movie has to do with having purpose, even in a situation where it is impossible to have a personal history.

Making Sense of the Film

It's helpful to understand that there is some rhyme and reason to the way events are portrayed on the screen in *Memento*. The film goes back and forth between color and black-and-white sequences. Those that are filmed color are shown backwards in time. The black-and-white sequences generally portray instances where Leonard is remembering his former life and, quite often, he is recollecting them on the telephone, though whom he is speaking to is never revealed.

Leonard has devised a system that he believes will allow him to keep track of what's going on in his life and to pursue a man he believes participated in the rape and murder of his wife. He writes notes, takes Polaroid pictures and captions them and, when a piece of information is particularly important, he tattoos it on his body so that he doesn't forget it. His notes, however, are somewhat cryptic and it is apparent during the film that there are times when Leonard isn't exactly sure what he meant to convey to himself when he wrote a note. Additionally, the film makes great use of conflicting information. Leonard has pictures, for instance, that indicate that certain people are lying to him, though there are instances when believing one of them would indicate that one of them is actually truthful and the other is a liar rather than both of them being liars.

Memento, in this regard, succeeds as a very effective psychological thriller. Like the protagonist, the audience feels disoriented, like they aren't exactly sure what is going on at any given time and, of course, that there is some sort of danger looming over the protagonist at every point during this film. This is an excellent film in regards to letting the audience experience what it's like to never know exactly who your friends and who your enemies are and what either of them might be manipulating you into doing.

Leonard's Quest

Leonard is trying to track down a man whom he only knows as John G. He believes that this man was involved in the attack in which his wife was raped and murdered. He claims that when he conveyed this to the police they didn't believe him and he has subsequently been trying to locate the man on his own since the incident.

During the film, Leonard constantly compares his condition with that of a man named Sammy Jankis. Jankis suffered from anterograde amnesia as well, and Leonard was tasked with investigating whether or not Jankis was faking his condition. Before the attack on his wife, Leonard worked as an insurance investigator. Through a series of tests, Leonard was eventually able to establish that the condition that Jankis suffered from was psychological in nature, allowing the insurance company to avoid having to pay for his treatments.

Part of the reason that Leonard is able to keep going and that he suspects that he will eventually succeed in his quest is the fact that he has learned from Jankis and is trying to avoid falling prey to the same pitfalls that plagued that unfortunate man. Leonard's detailed notes and ability to keep himself organized are what he believes will allow him to eventually find the man who raped and murdered his wife and exact his revenge.

Leonard is aided in his quest by Natalie, a bartender, and a man he knows as Teddy, both of whom very much give off the vibe of having ulterior motives. They do, in fact, have ulterior motives and, as the plot reveals, both of them cruelly exploit Leonard's condition for their own ends.

The Femme Fatale

Natalie is the type of vicious person who immediately picks up on the fact that Leonard has a condition that she can exploit for her own benefit. At the same time, she is given ample reason to hate Leonard upon meeting him. Natalie was involved with a drug dealer and, when Natalie and Leonard first meet, Leonard is still wearing Natalie's boyfriend's clothes and driving her boyfriend's car. Obviously, given that Natalie's boyfriend hasn't shown up in a while, Leonard has a secret that he's either not telling or simply doesn't remember.

Natalie becomes absolutely masterful at exploiting Leonard. In fact, some of the most painful scenes in the movie—and those that elicit the greatest deal of sympathy for the protagonist—involve Natalie abusing him in various ways. One particularly cruel scene involves Natalie spitting into a glass of beer, getting a patron at the bar to do the same, having Leonard spit in the beer and then, minutes later, serving that same beer to Leonard, well aware of the fact that Leonard will have no recollection of any of them spitting in it.

She also manages to anger him to the point where he strikes her, runs out of her house and sits in her car for a few minutes, and then comes back in claiming that a man named Dodd beat her—who she

The Thrillers

maintains is her boyfriend—and that she needs Leonard to get him out of town. One of the tensest sequences in the film takes place during this scenario, with Leonard frantically trying to write down the fact that Natalie just manipulated him before she comes back into the house, completely distracts him, leaving him without any memory of the incident at all.

Natalie baits Leonard along, getting information on John G for him from a friend of hers at the DMV. Unfortunately for the character named Teddy, Natalie gives Leonard a copy of a driver's license belonging to John Edward Gammell, Teddy's real name, as Teddy is an alias he uses in his work as an undercover police officer.

To make things even more confusing, Leonard has written a warning not to believe Teddy's lies on a picture of Teddy. In a later scene, Teddy warns Leonard not to believe Natalie, as she is the one lying to him.

How This Film Succeeds

As one can see from the setup already, a great deal of *Memento* has to do with confusion. Leonard is never exactly certain who his friends are and who his enemies are and why they might be one or the other.

The film also succeeds because it has that constant timer in it. While many thriller films rely on this plot device—*Taken*, for instance, gives the protagonist approximately 96 hours to rescue his daughter—the countdown clock in *Memento* is always there. Leonard has a brain condition that is inescapable and the consequences of it mean that his life is always a race against time to write down whatever just happened to him before he forgets it forever.

In some ways, Leonard is a character that exists halfway between living and dead. He has a history, but he has no present. He has a goal toward which he is working, but he is forever unable to realize how much progress he has made or if he has made any at all. Moreover, as characters in the film point out, if he were ever to succeed and take revenge upon the man who raped and murdered his wife, Leonard would simply forget it the next day. As soon as he closes his eyes, everything that happened to him while he was awake just fades.

There are also some great uses of ambiguity in the film. For instance, Leonard is shown many times talking on the phone—in black-and-white sequences—and giving an exceptionally detailed account of his life before his accident. In one scene, he looks at his arm and finds a tattoo that reads, "Never answer the phone." These little moments of realization add a lot of what amount to startle thrills to *Memento*. In many regards, they make the film interesting as, like Leonard, the audience is never certain whether or not someone or something that appears to be beneficial is actually a threat and, to some extent, the audience never really knows why anything is happening the way it is. The fact that the film—in its color sequences—unfolds backwards chronologically only increases this effect and is part of what made it so engaging for audiences.

The Plot Unfolds, but Not Clearly

As the film progresses, the sequences become more and more dreamlike. The backward chronology of the film allows the audience to piece together what has already happened, just as Leonard does. One of the things that makes this character particularly sympathetic, however, is the fact that he does this every single day. The audience only has to go through this ordeal once. Every morning, when Leonard wakes up, he has to figure out where he is, who he is with, who his friends are and, in some cases, has to figure out why there is a man beaten within an inch of his life stuffed into his closet.

Teddy is a very well-portrayed character who comes off as somewhat menacing and somewhat comforting at the same time. He understands Leonard and, as he states, Leonard has told Teddy about his condition over and over again. This device is played up throughout the film, where Leonard apologetically explains that he can't remember anything to characters who remember Leonard and, further, who remember Leonard telling them about his condition already.

The fact that Leonard is after a man he only knows as John G also adds tension to the film. The name is so common that it's inevitable that many people are going to match that description. In fact, Teddy's real name is John G. This will become particularly relevant at the climax of the film.

It becomes apparent to the audience, if not exactly apparent to Leonard, that he is being manipulated in many different ways. There are so many different types of crosses going on in this film that the terms double-cross and triple-cross really cease to have any meaning whatsoever. In the end, what the other main characters have told Leonard already turns out to be precisely true.

John G happens to be a name shared by Natalie's boyfriend. His real name is Jimmy Grantz and, just as Natalie had made clear, he is a drug dealer. Teddy sets up a meeting between the two, claiming that this is the John G that Leonard is looking for. In reality, Jimmy has brought $200,000 with him and Teddy has set up the murder so that he and Leonard can split the cash.

The film gets even stranger at this point. Teddy does turn out to be, at least relative to some of the other characters in the film, a good guy. After the attack, he actually believed Leonard when Leonard said that there was a second attacker and helped him to track him down. Leonard exacted his revenge, killing the second attacker but, just as Teddy told him, Leonard has no recollection of ever having done so. The entire hunt for John G since then is something that Leonard has conceived to give his life purpose.

It is also revealed that Jankis is not the person who Leonard believes. Jankis never had a wife. In a particularly painful scene in the movie, Jankis'wife tries to get Jankis to reveal himself as a liar by having him administer her diabetic injections over and over again. Because Jankis, whatever the cause, really cannot remember what he just did, he complies and gives her injection after injection of insulin. His wife eventually falls into a coma and dies. At the end, we find out that Jankis never had a wife. Leonard's wife, however, did survive the attack and was tormented by Leonard's condition. In reality, Leonard killed his wife. He killed his wife because of his condition and because she tried to get him to reveal that it was a pretense by having him give her insulin injections over and over again.

Faced with this reality, Leonard continues doing what he has been doing for the last year. He writes down Teddy's license plate number, leaves clues that indicate that Teddy is the John G that he is looking for and, thereby, explains why, at the beginning of the film, Leonard kills Teddy. Teddy happens to be a John G and, as far as Leonard is concerned, he will work just fine as the next subject of his quest.

Mental Illness in Thrillers

Part of what's going on with Leonard is a mirror of what goes on in the film *Gaslight*. People are manipulating him mentally to take advantage of him in some way. Additionally, the audience is never quite clear whether Leonard is actually the good guy in this film. He is, after all, wearing the clothes and driving the car of a dead drug dealer, involved with a cop who seems shady from the get-go and is involved with a woman who is obviously cruel and has something against him.

In many such films, it is ultimately revealed that the person being victimized is, in fact, someone that the audience can feel sympathy for. At the end of *Memento*, however, it is revealed that things are not only different than they seem as far as the supporting cast of characters go, but that things are much different with the protagonist than we have been led to believe. This film sets us up to believe that we are watching a man trying to exact vengeance on the killers who took his wife away from him while he suffers from a debilitating brain condition. In the end, what we find is that this man is really just trying to give himself purpose and, as much as any of the other characters, he is willing to sacrifice other people to his ends.

Memento has a 92 percent rating among critics and filmgoers on Rotten Tomatoes. It deserves this rating in every regard. The film not only succeeds in creating an air of tension, it also does what the best thrillers out there do. It allows the audience to feel afraid, uncomfortable and conflicted in a safe environment but in one that isn't so fantastical that the audience can't relate. For any fan of psychological thrillers, watching Leonard track down the killer of his wife—no matter how ironic that may turn out to be— is a great ride and one that's worth watching again, simply to pick up on the subtleties of this film and how masterfully it misdirects the audience as to what is actually going on.

http://www.simplypsychology.org/anterograde-amnesia.html

http://www.rottentomatoes.com/m/memento/

Taken (2008)

Director: Pierre Morel

Starring: Liam Neeson

Maggie Grace

Famke Janssen

Bryan Mills is a retired CIA agent who has a difficult relationship with his daughter. His daughter loves him, but Bryan has a tough time of it dealing with his ex-wife and her new husband. This all sounds pretty conventional thus far and, in fact, part of the reason that this thriller works so well is because it's set up in this way. There are plenty of retired intelligence workers in the world. Plenty of them probably have ex-spouses, too, given that their line of work tends to be pretty demanding. Not everyone who worked in intelligence is a well-trained, highly experienced killer who likely has an intelligence level comfortably in the genius range. For Bryan Mills, all of those things are true. If he threatens to look for you, find you and kill you, he's probably already at your front door and you're probably already as good as dead.

What makes this film work is that it is about people who are caught up in a particularly bad situation, some of whom have a particular set of skills...

The Setup

This film is directed by French director Pierre Morel. This lends it some unique style elements that make it feel a bit European, but the action will be familiar to anyone who is a fan of American action/thriller films.

The setup for the story in *Taken* really isn't groundbreaking in any way. Mills (Neeson) is apparently living a rather lonely life, but he's going to his daughter's birthday party and seems to revel in that. He gets her a karaoke machine. Her stepfather, after it is established that Mills is chilly with his ex-wife, gives Mills' daughter a horse.

Mills is getting upstaged. His daughter genuinely seems to love him, however, so the drama hasn't been turned up so high that the film risks being sidetracked by a too-conventional plot. Mills' daughter wants to head off to Europe, but Mills doesn't want her to go because he's afraid of what might happen to her. His overprotectiveness gives a clue as to what this man has done for a living, since he seems to be well-acquainted with how horrible the world can be for the unprepared.

It isn't long before his daughter and her friend are conned into giving up where they're staying, that they're alone and other vital information to a scout for a gang of Albanian human traffickers. In one of the first scenes where we see how cool-headed Mills is, he speaks to his daughter on her cell phone while she hides from kidnappers who have invaded her friend's apartment. Mills is an ocean away, but he keeps his cool and enlists his daughter as a way to start tracking the kidnappers. This rather establishes his character. The kidnappers haven't even found his daughter under the bed yet and Mills is already working out how to find them once they do kidnap her.

He tells his daughter to yell out descriptions of the men, leaving her phone under the bed so he can hear. Mills already has recording gear on his end of the phone call. She does what he asked as she's pulled out from under the bed, giving Mills enough information to start his search. When one of the kidnappers finds the phone, picks it up and puts it to his ear to see who's on the other end, he gets what amounts to one of the best You Are So Dead monologues in movie history, and one that's worth reproducing here:

> "I don't know who you are. I don't know what you want. If you are looking for ransom, I can tell you I don't have money. But what I do have are a very particular set of skills; skills I have acquired over a

very long career. Skills that make me a nightmare for people like you. If you let my daughter go now, that'll be the end of it. I will not look for you, I will not pursue you. But if you don't, I will look for you, I will find you, and I will kill you."

The criminal wishes Mills "Good luck." Even wishing Mills good luck is giving the retired agent a good part of the information he needs to kill you, as this particular criminal will find out as the movie gets going.

The Bad Guys Are Bad, the Good Guys Are Worse

Some of the criticisms of *Taken* claim that it's really just a dad-gone-wild fantasy. Others criticize it for being conventional and for being very derivative. In some regards, this may be true, but that doesn't take away from the quality thriller story that lies at the heart of this film, a bit conventional though it may be. True enough, it does have the bad-ass good guy appeal of the *007* franchise and it certainly does hinge on a tough guy rescuing a damsel in distress, though the damsel in this case is his daughter rather than his love interest.

Taken is interesting in that it allows the audience to take a trip to some of the darkest parts of life and, moreover, those parts of life that tend to look safe on the surface. Mills is an overly protective father, but he has a history as an intelligence agent and he works security for celebrities, so he likely has some good reasons to feel protective, given what he knows about the world. He's already been to that darker place and, in fact, seems quite comfortable there, as we see during the unfolding of the film. We see the nice, kind of tough but ultimately good father figure descend into what has to be one of the most murderous on-screen rampages of the 2000s outside of horror films or all-out action flicks.

We also see the dark side of Europe, which is usually not how the continent is cast in films, particularly American films. Generally seen as a cleaner, safer place to be than the US, the Europe of *Taken* whisks the audience away to a horrible, terrifying underground where human beings are sold like cattle to whoever is willing to pay the highest price.

The good guy is worse than the bad guys in this film as far as having the ability to kill quickly, efficiently and mercilessly. The bad guys, however, are so repulsive that it allows the audience to relax and enjoy seeing Mills knock them off one by one.

Mills may, indeed, be a dad gone wild, but he's gone wild for a good reason, the people he's losing it on have it coming and, ultimately, the audience knows that the longer that these people have his daughter the worse it's going to be for the criminals who kidnapped and sold her.

The Violence

It probably is easier to believe that the younger, more well-muscled heroes in most spy thrillers would be able to cut their way through a slew of baddies than it is to believe that Mills, who is clearly older, would be able to do the same. Some critics have pointed this out as making the film unbelievable at a certain level. The action is certainly over the top at times, but it works in the context of the film.

When Bryan Mills encounters enemies, he doesn't kill them, he assassinates them, basically to their face. He does cut through them like they were so much cheese and, to an extent, that's the point. These guys have bitten off way more than they could chew and things have finally caught up with them. To get out of the naysayer frame of mind and enjoy the film, note the following in terms of how the way the action unfolds:

Mills always uses any weapon he can, rather than heroically beating villains down in the manliest way possible.

Mills is not acting as a force for justice, he's acting out of revenge. Remember that he doesn't assume that his daughter will still be alive when he catches up to the kidnapper he talks to on the phone. He doesn't say he will find them, kill them and get his daughter back.

He may never get his daughter back and he knows it. He's still coming for the kidnappers.

Some of the reviews get things <u>wrong</u>, particularly when they're claiming plot conveniences. The Observer.com review says that the phone he threatens the kidnappers on "just happens to be lying under the bed where his daughter is hiding." The reviewer apparently just got back from the popcorn counter when they saw the scene, because they missed quite a bit of setup.

The action in this film is actually done quite well. Mills outwits his opponents by taking cover, keeping a cool head and setting up a string of hasty ambushes in many of the action scenes. He doesn't just shoot a thug and assume the thug dies. He shoots them several times, generally two or three times in the chest, the same way people who work in protection, law enforcement and related fields are trained to shoot.

Does *Taken* stretch the bounds of belief in some regards? Yes. Bryan Mills is surprisingly healthy after he's killed off many, many people, all of whom are killers themselves. None of this, however, really detracts from the film. Nitpicking aside, this film has a lot to offer in the way of tension and, when the violence does start up, it is fast, ugly and, in the case of what Mills does, within the realm of justification. This all makes for a great action thriller.

The Drama Unfolds

The people who have taken Bryan Mills' daughter, Kim, are very, very bad. Their method of keeping the girls in line is getting them addicted to drugs. Bryan knows he has 96 hours to find his daughter, starting the clock for the audience and ensuring that there is tension underlying the entire film.

Some of the victims of the kidnappers, such as Kim's friend, end up dying in their captivity. The conditions under which the victims are kept—at least those not sold to the highest bidder yet—are abysmal, which the audience first sees when Mills infiltrates one of their operations at a construction site. Seeing this sends him on a rampage, killing the thugs right and left and really only pausing when he has to kill one of them hand-to-hand and then moving almost casually—chillingly, really—on to the next. While prior scenes do establish quite well that Mills is a very dangerous man, this scene drives the point home. The villains, attempting to defend their turf, are simply outclassed. Mills dispatches them as if they were so many cockroaches to be stepped on.

Mills makes his way to a house where one of the construction site abductees has directed him. Earlier in the film, he gets some assistance from a friend who used to work for the French intelligence agency and, using his card, bluffs his way into the house. What follows is a great example of how an action thriller can deliver on its promise of tension and fear and still keep the action component that—literally, according to some reporting about this movie—can sometimes get an audience to their feet and cheering.

The scene that takes place in the house, with higher-level thugs than those that Mills has already executed, provides tension by placing Mills in a situation where he has to keep up a front long enough to get the information he wants. He poses as a corrupt intelligence officer and bargains with the thugs for a cut of their operation. Of course, in doing so, the thugs are giving Mills the information he needs. The fuse is lit. A piece of paper is what sets off the ticking time bomb that is Mills at this point.

He recognizes—or is relatively certain he does—the voice of one of the thugs at the table. He hands the thug a piece of paper with Albanian writing on it and asks the thug to translate it for him.

"Good luck."

From there, it's a slaughter. Mills dispatches the thugs in the house as efficiently as he did the others. If anything, he becomes more brutal. He's not letting anyone out of the house alive at this point and, after seeing the scene at the construction site, who could blame him? He begins gunning down the men in a running battle through the kitchen and the rest of the home that is so masterfully choreographed that the audience can give themselves permission to forget that, in reality, one man by himself would have likely been gunned down rather quickly. Not Mills. He even goes as far as using the bodies of the men he's already killed to shield himself from others, again using the hasty ambush tactics and blinding bursts of violence that are, by this point, the trademarks of his style.

Speaking of style, the personal style that Neeson lends Mills is part of what makes this character work.

Mills—Neeson—because he doesn't look the part of the international spy, is easy to sympathize with. He certainly doesn't look like the one to mess with, but it's not apparent that he is at all as dangerous as is the case, which is perfect for a character who was supposed to have lived most of his life in the shadows.

While his particular set of skills does play into the movie, looking at the man you can see that those skills are from a former part of his life. He's older, has lines on his face that connote stress and hardship and, despite the fact that the character is physically no small customer, he really isn't as intimidating on the outside as the thugs he's pitted against. Particularly in the climactic battle scene with the top-level thug, the audience can believe that this character could get himself killed. Mills has lethal skills, but he really gets by on being smarter and more experienced than the thugs he's working with. They may be menacing, tough looking and genuinely intimidating, but they're amateurs compared to him.

The human traffickers are the types of guys who spend their lives in and out of jail, are probably guilty of thousands of crimes for which they never get caught and who exploit the innocence of others to make their way in life. Mills is clearly used to dealing with villains a notch above what these guys have to offer. The criminals may be dangerous and powerful, but Mills is a guy with training intended to make him a threat to the deadliest people in the world and the traffickers just don't measure up. Putting the traffickers up against Mills is akin to putting an amateur boxer up against a professional

MMA fighter. The amateur may get a few shots in and cause some pain but, in the end, they're going to make mistakes and the more experienced fighter is going to be ready for those mistakes and will exploit every single one of them.

The traffickers continue to make those mistakes.

Mills makes it to an auction where women are being sold off to the highest bidder. This sequence contains some of the violence that critics objected to, when Mills becomes an executioner rather than killing out of survival. Again, who can blame him? Who would want to believe that people such as these are allowed to exist? They're not allowed to exist for long once Mills finds them and the audience gets a nice, visceral feeling of vengeance out of watching him take them out.

Mills ends up getting engaged in a masterfully directed chase scene involving a luxury sports car and a yacht, eventually making his way onto the yacht where his daughter is being held captive by a wealthy Arab.

Mills fights his way through the Arab's henchmen in what is probably the most thrilling action sequence in the film. These aren't the garden-variety, low-level thugs that Mills has been killing right and left since he got to Paris. These are pros and it shows in how they operate. Mills, at this point, is relying on his experience and the way he takes them out shows that he's simply done this more than they have. Even though this bunch of gangsters may be in their physical primes, Mills has an intellect and cleverness to him that only comes with years of experience.

The final baddie Mills has to take out, in accordance with the convention that the final brute has to have the equivalent threat level of all brutes before him combined, does not disappoint. A very intense knife fight ensues, with both men having it out hand-to-hand in a fight that has the feel of a cross between an honor duel and a knife fight in the trenches of WWI.

Mills takes this final thug out, but not without sustaining some serious damage himself.

The final kill in this movie is brilliant. Even after the audience has thrilled to watching Mills take his revenge on a group of people who wholly deserve it, the way he offs the man who bought his daughter is chilling for how cold it is. At some level, there is the feeling that Mills pauses for a moment just so the final bad guy can feel a glimmer of hope that he might live, just before Mills executes him and embraces his daughter.

Why This Film Works

Taken has a 58 percent rating from critics and an 84 percent rating from audiences on Rotten Tomatoes. There is clearly some discrepancy here between what critics and audiences thought of this movie and it bears examining.

Taken doesn't work because it's a great film in the sense that critics consider films to be great. This isn't a Hitchcock thriller. It's a gritty, dark and brutal film about revenge. The characters aren't always realistic; the thugs are always pure evil and the hero is, well, not exactly good, but he always has the right intentions.

Neeson's character doesn't develop in this film to any significant degree. In fact, in the epilogue, we see him back at it in his role as a dad, trying to make his daughter's dreams come true. The point of this film, however, is that none of that is the point. The point is to take the audience on a ride through some of the most intimidating and outright terrifying sides of life and Mills is the perfect guide. He does what he has to do because he has no choice. We don't see him for one second regret any killing he engages in. The authorities—it isn't long before the Paris authorities are aware that there is something going on—are merely foils to show the audience how good Mills is at evading detection and capture, good qualities in a former espionage agent.

Mills doesn't evolve because he's thrust into a situation that he's already adapted to. His job, as much as he describes it, was as a "preventer." He prevented bad things from happening in his former life. His retirement life turns out to put a tragically appropriate situation in front of him so he can use those skills once again. There isn't any reason for him to evolve. This movie is about someone being in a situation that calls for them to do what they do best. Mills does it very well. Neeson is flawless in this film and, despite the fact that critics have a problem with this movie, the audience approval numbers demonstrate that it's well worth watching and that, in fact, you'll probably watch it more than once.

In the end, *Taken* is really about how there are bad people in the world, but also that there are good people who are just as adept, and sometimes even more so, at using violence to protect those the bad people would exploit. For as dark as this film can be, it is, ultimately, hopeful.

http://observer.com/2009/02/dads-gone-wild/

http://www.rottentomatoes.com/m/taken/

For Further Sweating

If you want to stay on the roller coaster and keep the thrills coming, here are some films that will help you do that. Some of them cross into other genres, such as horror, but they still maintain the core of a thriller.

Inception (2010): A sci-fi thriller with a dense plot, great pacing and plenty of mind-bending effects. It will keep you engaged from beginning to end and will very much appeal to sci-fi fans who want to branch out a bit.

The Birds (1963): Avians go wild in this Hitchcock thriller. It's humans versus nature and the results are terrifying. You'll certainly think twice about running under that birdhouse after you see this film.

Psycho (1960): Black and white and dark as night; *Psycho* is relentless. This genre-defining film not only forever changed thriller movies, it also inaugurated the modern form of horror in its brutal depictions of violence and its terrifying portrayal of insanity.

The Machinist (2004): Take another ride into insanity with a man who cannot fall asleep. A great film for those who like the mind-screw end of things.

Black Swan (2010). Another film dealing with themes of insanity and, particularly, identity. This did very well with critics and stars Natalie Portman, who always knows how to make a good script even better.

Duel (1971): A semi-truck throws its weight around in this early '70s television movie and the results are thrilling. This is a very early Spielberg film and it's quite effective.

Taxi Driver (1976): A creepy chronicle of a man's breakdown amidst the crime-ridden warzone that was New York in the 1970s. Everyone knows the scene where De Niro wants to know if you're talking to him, but this Scorsese film has much more to offer than one good scene.

The Game (1997): Tight and effective, this movie features the pastimes of the rich and famous gone horribly wrong, with seriously tense results.

Bound (1996): A crime-caper/thriller involving two women trying to steal from one of their husbands, who happens to be a criminal himself.

There are many other fine films to choose from in this genre. If you've outgrown slashers and horror and still want that chill down your spine, look no further than thrillers!

Photo Credits

The photographs contained in this book are the property of their respective studios and may not be reproduced without express permission from the studios for any reason other than fair use as guided by copyright laws.

The origin source information is provided out of courtesy to the host of these pictures and any and all credits due the photographer should be displayed at these locations.

In order by photograph:

Source: Screenshot, public domain

Source: http://en.wikipedia.org/wiki/File:Yellowwp_med.jpg

www.ingramcontent.com/pod-product-compliance
Lightning Source LLC
Chambersburg PA
CBHW061645040426

42446CB00010B/1595